In Memory of
Hollie Marie Calhoun Miller
August 12, 1975-April 11, 1997

400 HOURS

A Father's Journal of His Daughter's Kidnap and Murder

Keith Benton Calhoun

Graystone PUBLISHING

Puckett, Mississippi

1st Printing, March 1999

10 9 8 7 6 5 4 3 2 1

Printed in the United States of America

Graystone Publishing Company
Phone Toll Free 1-888-455-5673
Fax (601) 825-1312
P.O. Box 10, Puckett, MS 39151
Online GSPublish@aol.com

Cover design by Lightbourne

Publisher's Cataloging-in-Publication
(Provided by Quality Books, Inc.)
Calhoun, Keith Benton
    400 hours : a father's journal of his daughter's
kidnap and murder / Keith Benton Calhoun. -- 1st ed.
    p. cm.
    LCCN: 98-73414
    ISBN: 0-9663078-2-8
    1. Murder--Arkansas--Texarkana. 2. Calhoun, Keith Benton.
3. Fathers of murder victims--Biography. 4. Miller, Hollie Marie
Calhoun, 1975-1997--Kidnapping, 1997. I. Title.

HV6534.A8C35 1999   364.15"23"0976756
                           QB198-1566

Acknowledgments

Writing this book was a very emotional experience for me. Because the contents are so personal and because it was my first attempt to communicate in this way, I was very apprehensive. I would like to thank Melanie Dotson for her assistance with the editing. I would like to thank Carol Cox for editing on such a professional level, while showing so much compassion for me and my writing; this was very reassuring for me.

Shortly after Hollie's death, Dr. Patrick McLain helped me to understand that my healing would be a continuous process and not a point that I would reach; I appreciate his guidance. Writing this book has helped me deal with issues that I might not otherwise have been able to. It has allowed me to realize that I could survive the devastation of losing a child in such a way and has given me the opportunity to show the reader a small part of who Hollie was and why we love her. Without Judi McLain's patience, understanding, and many hours of work on the book, none of this would have been possible.

Author's Note

I would like to thank the following: the Texarkana police department for their dedication and the long hours they put in searching for Hollie; the local FBI in Texarkana; the administration at Georgia Pacific for providing us with housing and support during the search for Hollie; the employees at Georgia Pacific and the people of Texarkana for their prayers and help; the Texarkana press and TV stations for keeping Hollie's picture in everyone's mind until she was found; the people who recognized Hollie's personal belongings, which led to her murderer; everyone who participated in the search for Hollie after the murderer was apprehended. I am grateful to the team of prosecutors who successfully indicted and convicted Hollie's killer.

I thank the *Texarkana Gazette* for permission to reprint the articles that appear in this book.

CONTENTS

PART ONE

The Last Talk

April 21, 1997

It had been two and a half weeks. We had become accustomed to moving around, not sleeping, and eating only when it became absolutely necessary. We never unpacked.

Linda, my wife, and I decided to go out somewhere to eat lunch. We got in the car, drove around to the front of the motel, parked, and went into the motel restaurant. That seemed far enough away for us to go.

When we finished lunch we drove around to the back and went to our room. Then we walked into the motel's conference room together. Linda's brother, Marvin, and his wife, Wanda, were there. Lt. Satterfield was sitting at the small table across the room with Marvin. As we went in he and Marvin stood up. Wanda was sitting on the sofa at one side of the room.

The lieutenant said, "Hello, Keith, Mrs. Calhoun..." As I walked across the room to shake his hand I thought, "He looks good today. Well dressed. Dark gray suit. Very shiny black shoes. He looks somewhat at ease—almost a reverse of the last time we saw him." I thought—"*It's over. He has found Hollie, and it is over.*" I didn't feel anything, except that I knew it was over, and that we could take her home now. *God, this was so hard.*

The lieutenant said, "*We have found what we think to be Hollie. We are 99 percent sure that we have found her.*" Linda was standing beside me. As he was saying, "I think we have found her," I saw Linda lean over and turn to leave the room. I never took my eyes off the lieutenant, but I could see her go, and Marvin went also. I was sorry that I couldn't be with her, but I couldn't leave just then.

I sat down at the table with the lieutenant and told Wanda she did not have to stay, but she did. I asked how long the murderer had had Hollie before he killed her. The lieutenant replied that the murderer had said that he had killed her the same afternoon he had taken her. *He must have had her for three or four hours.* I asked the lieutenant if he believed what this murderer had told him, and he said yes, given the other information that they knew was correct, or at least that they knew the murderer wasn't lying about.

The lieutenant told us that he had angered a lot of people in Cass County, Texas, because he wouldn't let them have this murderer. He also said that before I left I should make sure it was a federal case so it would be handled properly.

Hollie's husband, Jason, and his mother, Diane, came in

shortly after that, and the lieutenant told them. I think Jason wanted to know whether she had been raped. It was strange, but at the time it made no difference to me. *The fact that she was dead seemed to overshadow everything.*

I thanked the lieutenant for doing what he had said he would do, and he left with Jason.

September 20, 1997

When I started writing this I thought that perhaps I would find some strength in the process, or, if not, that at least writing it down would allow me to forget it for a while.

I have provided few physical details, and have written mainly about feelings. I haven't tried to explain everyone's actions. It was interesting to note how people looked at me and what their reactions were, and that has become much easier to talk about as time has moved along.

I thought that I would find some strength in people like Lt. Satterfield. He was someone for me to trust, and that meant so much at the time. *I realize now, however, that the only strength came from the fact that we survived the ordeal.*

The things that I kept thinking about do not bother me nearly as much since I finished writing about it all. I have developed a real appreciation for people who have a gift for writing and can make the reader feel what they feel or see what they see.

Now I have to go forth and deal with the murderer. I think I can do that. I'm glad it has taken this long. I needed the time to find myself and some parts of Hollie I couldn't quite understand.

October 11, 1997

This is my second attempt to write about our ordeal. The first time was last June, and it was too soon. It has been six months since Hollie disappeared. *That was on Friday, April 11, 1997.*

The last time I talked to Hollie was the Saturday night before *that* Friday. She had been to Mississippi State University for a shower and came down to our home in Madison on Saturday afternoon. I was working and didn't see her until that night. We had eaten late, and Linda and Hollie talked for a while. Linda went to bed about ten o'clock and Hollie and I sat up until one or one-thirty just talking and watching TV. I do remember the things we talked about. *I would like to remember every word that was said, but I can't.*

Hollie had spent the night before with her old buddies at

State, and I think she was missing that life to some extent. When she had what she considered a problem she used me as a sounding board. She would ask me for advice that we both understood would simply give her another perspective. Sometimes she would take it and sometimes she wouldn't.

That night she wanted to talk about school, Jason, and life in general. She was having a hard time in Texarkana, because the schools there did not have a social work curriculum. Jason and I had talked her into changing her major to business. She was making good grades, but she was not carried away with the world of business. We talked about her taking master's level courses in Texas, but I really didn't want her to do that, because it was such a long commute. She wished, I think, that she had finished at State before moving. I told her that she could go back to State or Ole Miss, but that would mean leaving Jason in Arkansas, which seemed to end her thinking in that direction. She did love Jason. We decided, after a very lengthy conversation, that she would have to make her adjustments in Arkansas so she could be with him. To her, there was really no alternative.

Hollie had met Jason her freshman year at MSU, and they had started dating the next year. Jason always saved Hollie and her friend a place at the State basketball games, which at that time was not easy to do. (State went to the Final Four the next year.) Jason would camp out for tickets, and Hollie would take coffee to him and his buddies on those cold nights while they waited for the windows to open. Hollie transferred to Ole Miss her junior year because State did not then have an accredited social work department. Most of her year at Ole Miss was spent going back to Mississippi State to see Jason. Linda and I were exhausted with worry because they were on the highway so much. When Jason graduated that year, he asked us if he could marry Hollie.

Hollie had once told us that she did not plan to marry before she finished school. She was very career oriented and had planned to get her master's in social work before she married. When she met Jason she said he was "the one," and she did not intend to let him get away. Jason had gotten a job at Georgia Pacific in Ashelow, Arkansas, which is about twenty miles north of Texarkana. It is a large plant and was a great opportunity for him. Hollie decided that she could take some of the courses at a small college there. She felt she could make things work out for herself.

They were very excited planning their marriage and their move. Everything was changing for both of them. It was as if they were on a mission—they were so intense.

Hollie was adjusting to her life as a yuppie wife. She had become aware that it was very important to Jason that they fit into his corporate world. The idea of belonging to cliques was not as appealing to her as it was to Jason. She was smart enough to realize that this approach would mean advancements for him in the future, but it meant nothing to her personally. I believe that part of the adjustment they were going through was the difference in their ages. She was twenty and he was twenty-five, which does not seem like a lot, but he had been away from home for six years and she for only two. At this time in their lives that made some difference. She was almost too young to settle into these cliques. However, she did think there were some really nice people in their little circle. Most of them were Jason's age or a bit older, and most of them had children, so their interests were somewhat different from hers. But these didn't seem like problems that she couldn't handle.

Hollie was really tight with money, while Jason, I think, felt that he was making enough money to do almost anything. Neither of them had ever had a lot of money. Jason had been at State for six years and had, I believe, lived on beans and rice and tacos for most of that time. Two summers before, I had suggested that Hollie open a checking account. She was keeping most of her money in a fruit jar in her bedroom. (She was like my grandfather; she didn't like to have her money where she couldn't see it.)

I told Hollie that what they were going through was called growing pains. Jason wanted Hollie to have everything. He also wanted a bass boat, and bought one, a purchase Hollie did not embrace wholeheartedly. I think what made her especially mad about it was that everybody at Georgia Pacific had a boat—it seemed to be necessary if you wanted to be part of the clique.

Most of the people he worked with were serious fishermen, and Jason was also quite good. Hollie had told me a lot about the boat before they bought it. They asked me about the trailer hitch for their Blazer, wanting to know if I thought it would pull the boat. They both liked to talk about it, but Hollie never admitted that. After the purchase she always referred to it as the *"damn* boat" when we talked. One problem was the fact that Jason would take his buddies from work fishing with him. I told Hollie that what she needed to do was to tell him she wanted to go with him the next time he went. She said, "I think that is exactly what I will do!" *When the police were questioning me, one of them said, "Jason had bought a boat recently. What did Hollie think about it?" I never said "damn boat."* It seemed to me that the police were seeing the boat as an example of the discontent that existed in Jason and Hollie's marriage. They apparently thought that it indicated that Jason was spending too much money on his own needs and pleasures. Financial matters do cause couples to fight and, I suppose, in some cases to hurt each other. The police had determined that Hollie paid the bills and appeared to assume that the meaning of that situation was that Jason had no regard for her feelings and that she was continually trying to arrange their money so that she could cover all the bad spending habits he had developed. But this was not the case, especially regarding the boat. The boat was an important part of their lives, because they dealt with it together. The police were trying to fit it into a scenario.

I had watched the police touch every part of Hollie and Jason's life. Their garbage, their clothes, their beds, and the dishes were all either moved, touched, or photographed. I tried to keep in mind that this was part of the process of finding her.

The boat was different. To me, the boat was sacred. I knew everything there was to know about it—how much it had cost and what the banker had said when Jason talked to him about financing. It needed a paint job, but was in generally excellent condition according to everyone who knew about such matters. There were some little things that were not working, but Jason could fix them. It had taken a week to get the hitch on the old Blazer ready to pull the boat. I knew that one of the puppies loved to ride in front and one always went to sleep when they started to move on the water. I knew that Jason liked to see how fast it would go, but only for a short distance. To me the boat represented who they were. With Hollie not there, Jason appeared to have controlled everything related to buying and keeping it. It was as though he was so spoiled and out of control he had never considered her. If Jason had been the one missing, Hollie would have appeared to be a bitching and totally discontented young wife.

They were so funny about that boat. They either fussed, cussed, or laughed about it all the time. It was an intimate thing—no one had a right to go there and take that apart—not even the people who were trying to find her. It was part of who they were. They *were* a family.

I could not show the police how they were. I could not explain enough times or in enough ways that the situation was not as it appeared. I refused to talk to them about it in any way. The police only asked me once or twice about it and really didn't pursue it with me, but to me that was even one step too many. It was going too far—it was much too invasive.

Hollie told me that Jason worked the Georgia Pacific system very well, saying that she could never be that committed to a place she didn't own. I told her we had kept her down on the farm too long.

Jason's mother worked at the McRae's in Mobile, so that's where Jason and Hollie would buy their clothes. A few weeks before she disappeared they had spent the weekend there, and Jason had bought her some very nice clothes. When they stopped to see us on their way home after the shopping spree, Hollie modeled the clothes for us. She would walk through, and we would tell her that whatever she had on was just perfect for her. She would smile and say, "Jason bought these for me." They told us how long they had shopped and described some of the items they had not bought. The last thing she showed us was a full-length, black leather coat. She looked like a million dollars. I told them they were spending too much money, but they explained that Diane had gotten a great discount. That was the highlight of their trip. Hollie was standing in our living room dressed to kill in her matching everything and that beautiful coat. Jason, Linda, and I were in blue jeans, housecoats, etc., so we told her to go put her T-shirt and cap on because we were feeling intimidated. She laughed and sat down and talked about what a good deal they had gotten on the clothes.

Their car even looked good. Everything looked good—and everything was expensive. The only drawback was that they *never* had any money. I thought they were going to have to stumble through such problems on their own. I was trying very hard not to interfere with what they were doing. Maybe I should have, but I didn't think so at the time.

Diane was planning to move to Texarkana. I think Hollie was more concerned about her moving there than she told me. *I will never know.*

Hollie was glad to be here that last Saturday night, and we did talk about more than just her problems with her newly acquired role in life.

She said she had driven into Oklahoma by herself the week before to check out a school there. She told me about riding down a country road and seeing rolling hills and pastures that seemed to go on forever. She had stopped beside the road to watch two cowboys moving a herd of longhorn cattle across a big field into the sunset. They were riding paint horses and had two or three blue heeler dogs working the cattle across the hill.

As she described the scene, she waved her hands, trying to show me exactly what it had looked like. When she finished telling me about it she looked at me and said, "Is that Heaven or what?"

I told her that what I was seeing was a little girl with her Mississippi State hat on talking to me about cowboys and their dogs at one-thirty in the morning. I also told her that maybe I had influenced her too much somewhere along the line.

I had always had heelers or some kind of cow dogs when I was in Puckett, the small country town I came from. They always rode in the back of my truck, and they worked the cattle with me. Hollie had thought I needed a blue heeler to ride with me. I told her they would probably eat somebody's lap dog, so I couldn't have one here. She had gotten me a puppy anyway, and had given it to me in March. (I gave the puppy away about two weeks after her funeral. I didn't want it to get killed following our dog, Madison. *I didn't want to bury that puppy.*)

Hollie really liked the farm, and the way I was when we lived in Puckett. I was glad she felt that way.

I had worked hard all that Saturday, and I was tired. It was getting late. We both agreed we had better go to bed and try to get some sleep. *She did love to talk.*

The last time I saw Hollie was that Sunday morning. She left soon after we got up, so we didn't have time to talk very much. I can still see her in my mind, *going down the driveway. She had that little black hat on that Jason had gotten her in Mobile, and she had her hand out the window waving as she drove away for the last time.* We wanted her to leave early because we felt it was not safe for her to be on the road alone. Hindsight is a killer sometimes, isn't it? *I did love to hear the child talk.*

The day Hollie left for her freshman year at MSU, I went to fill her car with gas. When I returned, I found Linda in the kitchen preparing one more snack for Hollie's journey (after all, it was a two-hour drive and there might be nothing for her to eat later). I walked through the house and into Hollie's room, where she was standing surrounded by suitcases and boxes filled with all those little things that a freshman thinks that it would be impossible to live without. I told her that her car was waiting. She wanted to go alone, I think, because I had taken Weslea on her first day, and Hollie, of course, wanted to be more independent or at least different.

I looked around the room, laughing a little, and asked if she thought we could get all that in her car. We agreed that we could.

We looked at each other for a minute. Then I asked her if she was scared. She said, "Maybe a little." I said, "Yeah, me, too, a little." I kissed her forehead. Then we packed the car, and she left for her adventure.

PART TWO

The First Week

Friday, April 11, 1997

Morning

On the Friday she was kidnapped, she had called our house at 9:38. I came in at lunch and saw her number on the caller ID. I didn't call her back. She would always leave a message if she needed something—*so I did-n't call back. I just didn't call back. I won't go into what might be different if I had. I have already been there.*

Night

That night, Linda called Hollie's and Jason's house about eight just to chat. Jason told her that he didn't know where Hollie was. He said he thought she might have gone some-where with one of her friends. When Linda got off the phone she told me that Hollie was not there, and that Jason sounded worried. About thirty minutes later I called him back, and he told me that he had checked with the neighbors, but no one had seen her. He said he had called the police. I hung up, and Linda and I put some clothes and a few things together. I called back about nine, and the police were there. We told Jason to call us on the car phone if he heard anything from her. *We left.*

We started calling him as soon as we were on the road. It was about a five-hour drive. The later it got, the less frequently we called. As long as we weren't talking to Jason, I could convince myself that she was just out with a girlfriend or was at home by now. As time passed, however, this tactic worked less well for me. *It became a very long drive.* I kept thinking how totally out of character it was for her to leave, even for a little while. She and Jason went everywhere together. As I drove I began to imagine some of the things that could have happened to her; then I would quickly dismiss them and think how silly I was going to feel after we had come so far only to find her at home. The last time I called we were about twenty miles from Texarkana. By this time I had run out of places in my mind where she could safely be. *It was like accepting cold, hard fear by degrees—real fear.*

I hope that I will someday be able to forget the feeling I had when we walked into Hollie's house. Jason looked very hollow and tired, and I suppose we did, too. It was about three o'clock. He repeated what he had told the police about what he knew. He had found a blonde wig and a pack of cigarettes in the house when he got home. There was a pair of Hollie's panty hose tied in a knot lying on the table, and the telephone receiver was missing from one of their phones. None of us knew what to do or say, not even to each other. Jason could hardly talk. He would point to something like the phone, and try to tell us how or where it was when he got home. He would take a deep breath and talk in such a low voice that I could hardly hear him. He could only say it once. He had been sitting alone for six hours now, and as much as he tried it was really hard for him to explain each thing to us.

He acted as though we had given him something very precious to take care of and he had lost or misplaced it, but he couldn't really understand how that could happen, or why it would happen.

There seemed to be so much distance among the three of us. I tried to talk to him about what had happened that day. I asked about her friends. "Are you *sure* she couldn't be with one of them?" Talking to him was almost impossible, and he could hardly speak to me. It was as though we had never met. Without Hollie standing there we could not communicate with each other. I was unable to define it at the time. We just could not communicate. It was as if we were strangers.

Jason told us that there would be no detectives on duty until six a.m. Saturday. We decided we would lie down for a little while—physically I had taken about one step too many. I had to try and get some rest.

We just lay there. Linda cried some, and I think she went to sleep for a little while. *I could do nothing except stare at the ceiling and wonder where my child could be.* Jason was trying to sleep on the kitchen floor by the only phone left in the house. He did get some sleep. I don't remember closing my eyes. I don't believe I ever did. I kept thinking, *"I don't know where anything is here. I get lost easily here. Where am I going to look for her? I don't know where I am here."* After an hour or so, I had gone over in my mind everything that I thought could have possibly happened to her.

Sometime before the others woke up, I began to imagine her as an angel. When I tried to think of what she looked like, *I would see her only as an angel in a white robe, with long hair, smiling at me from somewhere above.*

I came to believe at that moment that she was dead, and that she was safe with God. I have thought over the last few months that my mind couldn't deal with the idea of what kind of pain she would most probably be in if she were alive. It was either that, or she and God had taken some mercy on me and let me know that she was in no pain. *I knew she was gone, and I knew I had to find her. We could not leave her here, with this as her final place.*

Her house was cold; it was always cold. We had visited only once before, in February, and it was cold then, too. Her puppies would sit around the floor furnace, and she would laugh at them. I never took my clothes off that night. I just lay there.

———

It was six months ago tonight that she disappeared. A few months back I would never have believed that I could sit in this chair and write the word "Hollie" or look at that chair where she sat and talked. I have written tonight for as long as we talked that last time. Sometimes I can feel her presence. I will always miss the talking. Good night, Hollie—love ya.

Saturday, April 12, 1997

Early Morning

After a night that seemed to go on forever, we found ourselves at the police station at six o'clock Saturday morning. This is where we had the pleasure of meeting Detective Hawkins. Hawkins had read the police report from the night before and decided that Hollie was a runaway. The more we tried to explain to him, the madder we got. He was always smiling at the wrong time; his behavior could not have been more inappropriate. The three of us could hardly say anything without tearing up and losing our voices. I would look at Jason and realize he could not say anything. Then I would try to talk, and start to cry—then stop. I felt as though I should be in control for Jason's and Linda's sake, but I could hardly speak. I finally asked Hawkins if there was any way we could convince anybody there that she hadn't run away.

Something was terribly wrong. He told me I needed to get some more evidence. I told him we were not cops. I didn't think hitting him would be productive. We left and went back to Hollie's.

The only thing I remember about getting to the house is standing in the front yard, looking around and wondering, *"Where the hell am I going to start looking? I'm lost here. So where the hell is Hollie?"*

Midmorning

I started calling people. I called my lawyer in Mississippi first. He asked me about Jason and about his and Hollie's relationship. He also told me to call the FBI and the sheriffs in some of the other counties.

When I called the FBI, I got a recording, which was very depressing. Then I started calling family members.

I would start to tell somebody at home that she had disappeared, but I would fall apart for a minute, so Linda would take the phone and start to talk. Then I would take the phone back and finish the conversation.

I have never been that mad. I was still preoccupied with Detective Hawkins. (He was the one who told us that twenty-four hours would have to pass before they could do anything.) He could have been the most dedicated policeman in the world, but the only thing he meant to me that day was that no one was interested in Hollie until the twenty-four hours was over. *There was no way we could survive the twenty-four hours without her.*

I left at least six messages with the FBI, and called all the hospitals, the highway patrol, etc. My lawyer told me that a private detective could not help this soon, and said that I needed to go door to door in Hollie's neighborhood asking people if they knew anything. That's all we could do for now. I kept thinking how long the twenty-four-hour wait would be. Jason had called Hollie's friends at some point. I spent at least an hour or so talking to the phone company trying to find out who she had called that day. At the time, it seemed important.

The older of my two daughters, Weslea (she was twenty-four then), had been married for about fifteen months to Martin, and they lived in Starkville, Mississippi. I called Weslea's father-in-law's house, talked to Martin, and told him to tell Weslea. I didn't feel comfortable having him be the one to tell her—I knew it would be hard for him—but I could not risk falling apart on the phone as I had done with everyone else. They were about six hours away, and I knew their trip would be hard enough as it was. She didn't need to hear me cry at that point.

Early Afternoon

Through the morning and early afternoon, people began to call back. I was still trying to call other people. Mostly what I remember is holding the phone talking to people who couldn't help, and looking around Hollie's kitchen thinking, *"There's nothing to eat in here. They must eat out every meal. There is a lot of cola in here. Those two puppies are always under my feet."*

I kept looking at that phone—the one that had no receiver—thinking, *what a strange thing to be missing.* It was very hard to put all of this together.

It was so cold here for April. I kept wondering if Hollie might be cold.

Linda didn't know what to do, so she cleaned up Hollie's bedroom. I told her this might not be a good thing to do. Jason just kind of walked in and out. He didn't say very much to anyone. He called his mom and some friends.

Some of Hollie and Jason's friends began to come by in the afternoon. They took some of Hollie's pictures so they could make flyers. *In the picture, she was smiling.*

I waited outside for Weslea all afternoon, worrying about her. When she got there she walked across the yard with her arms folded—*she looked cold.* She asked me if anything had changed. I told her nothing had. She seemed so frightened. After she had been there for a while, we went for a walk. I told Weslea I was worried about her, and I did not want her to lose faith no matter what happened or how we found Hollie. I told her that very bad things happened to very good people, and that God had not given Hollie up, or her either. Then, with desperation in my voice I said, "You can cuss everybody, even God, but please don't give him up."

I have decided since then that watching one of my children after the other one had disappeared gave me a feeling of wanting to hold on to Weslea. *I did not want to lose any part of her. I could not stand the thought of her changing in any way. "Please remain as you are, Weslea," I kept saying to myself as I was looking at her.* At the time I really believed I was helping her, but I think I was protecting myself. She was very strong and very focused on finding Hollie—much more so than I was.

Later that afternoon people from a local TV station showed up and began asking us questions about Hollie. I do not really know how they got there.

I remember talking to the anchorwoman, whose name was Jan, and who asked Linda and me how we were holding up so well. I thought, *"What are we supposed to do? I can't find anything here."* I remember watching her mouth as she talked. It was as though the sound were turned off and I was watching a close-up of her lips, not really hearing her. *She had the reddest lipstick I had ever seen. I thought, "Hollie really liked red lipstick."* There were cops everywhere—they seemed to just appear. *I thought about dark and wondered whether Hollie was surrounded by it.* Jan wanted to do an interview with Linda and me later that night. She also wanted to do one with Jason.

I was afraid that if someone had Hollie and heard the interview he might be crazy enough to get off on the news coverage. I asked her not to make it tacky. I think she was somewhat taken aback, but she was very understanding and seemed confident in her ability to produce a piece that would work and would not be tacky. I told her she would have to clear it with the police before she could put it on the air. I didn't know at the time her husband was the chief of police.

As Hollie would say, *"No problem there."*

Night

Jan did the interview much later that night. I remember sitting on the sofa with Linda. Jan had the microphone in my face. She asked me to describe Hollie, and I said,

— 29 —

"Sorry, I can't do that." Linda said, "We just want to know that she's all right." I just couldn't say anything about her.

Cops were in and out of the house. At some point I met Tom McCollum, the FBI agent who worked in that area. He was in his late thirties, and he was wearing blue jeans and Keds. He was very nice to all of us, and he talked directly to us when he spoke. After eighteen hours of knowing that something horrible had happened, I found that Tom's professional demeanor and intensity simply reaffirmed my worst fears. I asked him if he had gotten the messages I had left for him on his recorder. He seemed to be in charge of the investigation.

The puppies were having a great time—they thought everybody was there to play with them.

At one point Tom took me outside to his car so we could talk in private. He looked at me and said, "There are some things that are hard to talk about with the father." He asked me if I was close to Jason, and did I suspect Jason of doing *this?* I said, *"Doing what?"* He told me there was evidence of a crime. He did not say what. I looked at him and said, "It took me five hours to get here, and I suspect everybody in this damn place, including *you* and *Jason*."

Tom continued very calmly to ask me questions about personal matters in Hollie and Jason's life. It was much too intense, and it was hard for me to go from where I was sitting there with him to Hollie and Jason's daily routine. This was not a long conversation.

Later that night Tom asked me if I would help him go through some garbage bags that were out in the garage. I held his flashlight for him while he scrambled through the bags. I do believe that being part of that procedure led to one of the most sickening feelings I had experienced in my life up to that point. It was the beginning of the most invasive process with which I have ever been involved. Hollie was not an especially private person, but this was going much beyond privacy. Nothing was in the bags except papers and junk. There were bills Hollie had written on and pieces of paper with notes to herself and to Jason. Tom would get one of the pieces of paper out and ask me about it, and I could visualize Hollie writing it or paying or not paying that particular bill. It was like taking one step and being inside her life—*but she was not there.* He looked at every single item that was in the bags. I was thinking, *"Hollie moved some of this crap from home with her. She must have carried it with them."*

While we were going through the garbage I told Tom I could not help him prove that Jason had had anything to do with whatever had happened. I said that if Jason did have anything to do with it Hollie was dead for sure, because I couldn't imagine that he would leave her tied up somewhere for this long. I probably should not have said that to him; it could not have helped Jason much.

I asked Tom if he would search the attic in the house. I had looked up there earlier, but I couldn't see much. He took a couple of men, but did not find anything. I always felt funny about the attic, maybe because I had stared at the ceiling all the night before.

The puppies were everywhere, having a great time. They had fingerprint dust all over themselves and were constantly under the cops' feet. Jason decided it would be better to get them out of the way, so he took them to a friend's house for the night. When Tom realized Jason was gone, he became very upset. I assured him that Jason had only gone to take the puppies somewhere and that he would be back. I realized then that Jason was the target—*for real.* I didn't know what to do to help Jason.

When Jason got back, Tom told him they needed to get some information from him to clear up a few matters. They sat him down at the dining room table. Tom sat at the end of the table and Jason at the side; there was a detective on each side, and three more detectives standing around. *Hollie, her name was Hollie.*

It seemed like so many cops. As I watched them I remembered a scene from a movie video that Weslea had given me, in which someone had kidnapped a man's child. The FBI and police were all over his house and were asking him a lot of questions. He asked them why they were standing around talking to him in his house when it was clearly the one place on earth where the kid wasn't going to be found.

After everyone was in position, Jan asked if she could get an interview with Jason before they got started. They said it was O.K. Everyone remained in place while Jan set up the cameras and her equipment. Jason left the room and went into the bedroom for a few minutes. When he came back, he was crying. He sat down and she began; he cried on and off throughout the interview. The first thing he said was that he didn't know where Hollie was, and then he said that if someone out there had her please not to hurt her. I was amazed that he could speak so well. It was as though he had programmed himself, and this was getting him through the interview. *It seemed so wrong.* The fact that I had not been able to communicate with anyone on this level didn't enter my mind at the time. The detectives standing along the wall were behind Jan and were watching the interview. I thought, *"Jason, you are not helping yourself—if Hollie comes home she is going to kick your butt back to Mississippi."* The interview was not long, because Jan wanted to get it in for the six o'clock newscast, or maybe it was the ten o'clock; I can't remember.

The police started their interrogation of Jason. I kept thinking, *"I hope he knows this is an interrogation and not a chat."* Tom asked all the questions. He was sitting the closest to Jason.

Tom: "What time did you get home?"

Jason: "Three-thirty."

Tom: "Why did you buy two pizzas?"

Jason: "We always eat two."

Tom: "What time did you take a nap?"

Jason: "Four or five o'clock, I think. "

Tom: "When did you notice the panty hose tied in a knot?"

Jason:"I'm not sure when."

Tom: "Were they on the floor or the table?"

Jason:"The table."

Tom: "Do you always eat two pizzas?"

Jason:"Always."

Tom: "Just let me get this cleared up. What time did you take a nap? We need to get the time lines closer."

Jason:"Four or five."

Tom: "And you got home about—what time?"

Jason:"Three-thirty."

Tom: "You know those panty hose? Strange they were tied in a knot—you think so?"

Jason:"Yes."

Tom: "When you first saw them they were on the table, right?"

Jason:"I think so, on the table."

Tom: "Did you pick them up off the floor or were they already on the table?"

Jason:"I think on the table."

Tom: "You and Hollie eat out a lot, like everybody, I guess."

Jason:"Yeah."

Tom: "When did you see the wig?"

Jason:"When I came home."

Tom: "Does Hollie wear wigs?"

Jason:"No, not that I know of."

Tom: "Did you find that kind of strange or unusual— the wig on the floor?"

Jason:"Yeah."

Tom: "I need to get this panty hose thing cleared up— you picked them up off the floor and put them on the table. Is that right?"

Then, Tom asked Jason this about the panty hose—"If

you had them around your neck and they were tied so that you couldn't pull them over your head, how would you get them off?" Jason told him exactly in a very precise, step-by-step way, how you could get them over your head. It was as if he were tackling a math problem.

I don't know what time this started; it must have been about nine or ten o'clock. The interview lasted four or five hours. The police never moved, and never said anything except when Tom spoke to them to break the tension.

I sat in the recliner in the living room and watched and listened for three to four hours. Tom's pattern never altered. He would change subjects; then he would return to an earlier question. He was speaking in a casual manner as if he were having a normal conversation. It was very methodical, very calm, and very, very persistent.

At some point Linda went to sleep on the sofa. A woman taking pictures of the crime scene came through, but Linda never moved. The woman took a picture of her asleep on the sofa.

My feelings about what had happened to Hollie began to change after two or three hours of the interrogation. All the anger, shock, and initial fear from earlier that day began to be replaced by something much deeper, much harder, and unfortunately, much more real. This was a cold place to be.

I felt like I couldn't sit there any longer. I went out onto the porch and called my dad. I talked and talked. As long as I was talking, even if it was about the situation, I didn't have to *think* about it. Dad, a concerned father and grandfather, wanted to know every detail, but there were none. He told me that Robert Means and some other people from Puckett wanted to come up the next day. I said we appreciated it, but I didn't think they needed to come. I went on to tell him that we were dealing with it the best we could. I asked him to try and not worry so much about us, because we would be O.K. I just didn't think I could handle a lot of people hugging on me. He called back Sunday morning and told me that Prentiss (my first cousin on my dad's side) and Sandra (his wife) were bringing him. I thought that would be O.K. Prentiss is not really big on hugging.

Having been in shock all through Saturday while I was talking to the cops and trying to answer their questions, I think I had begun to develop a kind of detachment while dealing with them. I once saw an interview with Merlin Olsen in which he was asked how he could play football with such intensity, be such a ferocious competitor on the field, and then be so easygoing and laid-back off the field. He said that when you play it's as though you are outside yourself, with the intensity of the game rising. I felt as though our situation was similar but magnified about a thousand times. I knew that if someone who loved me and who also loved Hollie were to touch me, then that kind of detachment would disappear. During this period, Jason, Linda, Weslea, Diane, and I almost never touched or hugged each other. I think we knew that if we did, our minds would immediately be filled with thoughts of Hollie, and it would be so painful that we would not be able to function in any capacity. *At the time detachment was the only thing that worked for me.*

Sunday, April 13, 1997

Early Morning

I talked to Dad on the phone until Tom finished questioning Jason. It must have been about two or three o'clock Sunday morning.

Tom came outside where I was and told me they felt much better about Jason. He said, "Jason is O.K. We needed to get some of the facts straight, but we are pretty sure he is O.K. We have developed some more leads, and everyone in our department is working on the case." *Hollie—her name is Hollie.* I thanked him for putting so many people on it, and he left.

When he left, I was standing outside; it was a little warmer and it was not raining anymore. Hollie had been gone for two days now. I thought that if she was still alive she must be really strong, but two days is a long time to be strong.

I'm not sure where I slept the next few hours. I do remember that Linda slept on the sofa and Jason on the floor. I think I slept in the chair where I had been sitting and listening as they questioned Jason.

Sunday was the most emotional day for everyone; I think exhaustion must have had something to do with it. I don't remember having eaten anything on Saturday. I can only remember smoking and drinking Cokes almost constantly. It seemed that I never stopped talking, and my mouth was always dry and cottony. The cigars seemed to calm me to some extent so that I could talk and be coherent. People were calling on the phone almost constantly now. Caffeine and nicotine seemed to be all I needed to keep myself moving. What little eating was done would happen as someone passed the table. No one sat down to eat, and no two or three people ate at the same time. It was as though we were uncomfortable sitting together in one place.

Early Afternoon

Everyone who knew Hollie and Jason must have come by at some time during the day. The story had been on TV several times by Sunday afternoon. Jan made a story of everything; before the week was over, I had learned to appreciate her instincts. She had known from the beginning that something was very wrong here, even though there was little evidence that anything bad had happened. The kind of crime she seemed to suspect was not common in Texarkana. Maybe the information in the police report seemed as strange to her as it did to me. Hollie's picture was on TV every time the news was on.

Three of Hollie's friends came over. They had made
some flyers with her picture on them for us to give out. It
was a really good picture. The girls looked like slightly
older versions of Hollie. They wore caps most of the time.
They were very straightforward and organized. They
intended to find Hollie *that* day. Hollie had told me about
one of them. She was about twenty-seven or twenty-eight,
small, and she looked kind of like Kim, my younger sister.
She was very business-like and outspoken. I believe she
was a naval recruiter. She was so strong on that Sunday.
As the week wore on I think it became harder and harder
for her to look at me directly. She never did cry. I think it
was because she avoided talking to me for very long at
any one time. I thought that maybe she had known Hollie
better than the others had.

It seemed that all the people who knew Jason at work
came by Sunday. Everyone brought food. They told us
how sorry they were, and some of them prayed.

Hollie's mail carrier, a woman about forty years old,
walked through the house when no one was there. She said
she was psychic, and that there were bad spirits in the
house. I asked her if she was talking about herself. She did-
n't stay long, but she made a *real* impression.

It was as though Weslea had been in training for this
most of her life. She had met with Jason early that day
and begun planning interviews with different people. She
also helped Hollie's friends with the flyers they were distributing. She was always busy doing something to help
find her sister. At times she would ask me what she
should do, and I could only say, "*Stay focused—just stay
focused and do what you do best—talk to these people.*" Weslea

was impressive on TV because she could speak well—very well.

On Sunday the police came by and told Jason they wanted him to take a polygraph test Monday morning. They said they just wanted to clear up some things and eliminate him from the process. Jason was upset. I believe he thought that he had been cleared the night before, and that nothing else would be expected of him. I told him it was just part of the process. I couldn't really think of anything else to say to him at the time. This pretty much eliminated Tom from the list of people I could trust here. I was not in a frame of mind for someone to patronize me. However, Tom did bring us some sleeping bags. He was nice enough—just a bureaucrat trying to do a job.

Cops were all over the place Sunday afternoon, questioning the neighbors. When they talked to us I could tell they were still thinking that Hollie had walked out or that she and Jason had had an argument, or something like that. The hardest thing to deal with when I was talking to these people was the fact that none of them knew Hollie. *No one could see Hollie; she had lost her identity.* I couldn't describe her out loud, and I just couldn't understand why no one in the whole damn place could see her as she was. It would not be good if they were looking for a newlywed who had gotten mad and left. I couldn't seem to explain to them that she was not like that. *She just would not have done that—ever.* They needed to know what to eliminate from their thought processes.

I couldn't help thinking that Hollie would have done what she could have to handle any situation herself. This, I think, bothered me more than anything. I was afraid she

would not ask for help—not even from me. I knew that if
she was having problems here she would not have wanted
to worry me. We talked often, and I knew a lot about her
day-to-day problems, but I began to think that if she had
had a major one she might not have talked to me. Maybe I
had taught her too well. She could manipulate me, after
all. Not on a large scale—just day-to-day little things—but
if I didn't ask directly she probably would not tell me she
was having any major problems. I was getting to the point
where this was causing me a great deal of concern.
*Actually it scared the hell out of me—the idea that she could
have had something serious going on and not discussed it.*
Maybe not. I couldn't seem to hold my thoughts together
very well that Sunday. There were so many people and so
many police. *So many questions.* It was something of a
struggle for me just to walk around. None of these people
knew Hollie, but they were trying hard to help.

Sunday afternoon Linda and I went to buy groceries. It
must have been early in the afternoon, because no one had
brought anything over by that time. As we drove to the
store, every mile or so, we could see one of the flyers
Hollie's friends had made taped on a window. The girls
had done a good job of getting them out. I had already
seen the fliers, because the girls had brought them by after
they were printed to see what we thought and to make
sure we approved. But it wasn't the same now, seeing
them stuck to store windows. *This made it very real.* The
pictures were everywhere. We decided we could handle
this. We couldn't stay in all the time while we were here,
and she was missing.

As we parked the car, I could see a poster from across

the parking lot on the grocery store door. *I can do this— this doesn't bother me.* We walked up to it, looked, and went through the door— *no problem.* We were not in there for very long, buying only a few things. I left for the car first. I think Linda was looking at something behind me in the store.

The girls had been very thorough. They had put a flyer not only on the *in* door, but also on the *out* door—very efficient. This one was at eye level. I had not been expecting to see another one of those things until we were on the way home. Suddenly there it was about four feet away—*she was just looking back at me.* The door wouldn't open because *I couldn't seem to step onto the mat that would open it. I couldn't seem to move or breathe, or do anything except stand there and look at that picture. This couldn't be Hollie—not my daughter—not stuck to a door—not smiling so big—not missing. What the hell am I doing standing in a store? My child is missing! I have some food from a store in Arkansas, and my child is not here. She is so pretty. Where are you, Hollie? Why are we here? I can't be here.* I really don't know how long I stood there—probably not long. An elderly woman finally pushed past me, and the door opened. If I could have, I would have kissed her. The door had to move on its own. *I couldn't make it open.*

Going back to the house, Linda and I talked very little to each other. When we did speak it was to say that the flyers were necessary, that we had had to get food for the other people, that it was O.K. for us to leave the house for a little while.

When we got back with the groceries, Jan was there working on a story for the news. Some people from a local

HOPE
for Hollie

Missing Since
April 11, 1997 from
the area of Laurel
and 20th Street.

Age 21
Height 5'6"
Weight 140 lbs.
Brown Hair, Hazel Eyes

A Hollie Miller
Benefit Account
has been opened at
Texarkana National Bank.
Contributions can be
made at any TNB to
help with finding Hollie.

Any information please call
(903) 793-STOP or
(501) 774-7682

"I couldn't seem to move or breathe, or
do anything except stand there and look
at that picture. This couldn't be Hollie—
not my daughter—not stuck to a door—
not smiling so big—not missing."

cafe came by and brought some hamburgers and french fries. Jan finished the story she was working on, and then interviewed the owner of the cafe to make another story. She talked to us for a little while and left. She made these little stories out of everything. Good press—I suppose.

At some point that afternoon, when there were a lot of people in the house, I became emotional. I began to feel myself tearing up, so I walked out onto the porch, not crying, just needing to be outside. I was standing on the step when I saw a kid going from door to door handing out some kind of flyer. He was about twenty-five, wearing a white shirt and tie, and had blond hair cut short. He looked very neat. I thought he must be from a church.

When he walked up, I guess he could tell that something was not O.K. He introduced himself and told me he was an evangelist from the Baptist church down the street. He was filled with the love of God, and I believe he thought he could fix just about anything. He looked at me and said, "Is there anything I can do for anyone?" I just stood there for a minute looking back at him, and then I said, *"My daughter is missing. Her-name-is-Hollie."* I didn't cry, but I couldn't speak very well. He said, "Would you like for me to say a prayer for Hollie?" I nodded my head yes, and he began to pray. I stood there on the top step looking down at his shiny little head. He prayed and prayed. I think that he didn't want to stop praying because he didn't want to look back up at me. He finally stopped and he did look at me, and I felt as though I had taken all that was heavy from my own shoulders, and placed it on his. I thought, "Thank you, God, it's not as heavy for me right now. I am so sorry for this young man, but maybe he was sent here to share some of the weight for a short while." *I do know that I felt better.* I thanked him for stopping, and he went to the next house.

I think about him sometimes and wonder how he is doing. I will never forget the feeling I had as he prayed or his face when he looked up at me.

Late Afternoon

I was still standing on the front porch when Prentiss, Sandra, and Dad got there. They parked across the street in front of Hollie's house. A couple of policemen and some other people were standing in the yard. Dad was in the back seat of the car, and he got out first. He immediately started walking towards me, past the policemen and the others in the yard. It was as if we were the only ones there.

———

When I was in college a tornado hit my parents' home. I was in school, about three hours away. Someone called Linda and told her what had happened, but gave her very few details. As we were driving home, I imagined how the house might be damaged and how we might have to stay away from school for a little while to help repair it.

When we finally got home we had to park on the highway some distance from the house because there were so many people there. Patrolmen were directing traffic.

When I walked up and looked at the place where our house was supposed to be, I saw nothing but people standing in small groups and talking to each other. There was no house, only a bare spot where it had been. All the trees were gone; only twisted stumps were left. There was even a strip where the grass had been torn away by the tornado.

I stood there for a few seconds, and then I saw Dad walking across that bare spot and across the yard towards me. He was the only person I could see in the crowd of people. He looked tired, out of place, and for some reason older than he had the last time I had seen him, just a few days earlier. He walked up to me, and we shook hands. He told me that Mother and Kim were O.K., and then he smiled and said, "But the house needs a little work."

When Dad got to Hollie's house, he got out of the car and walked towards me, across the yard, through all those people, without speaking to anyone else, and shook my hand. I told him that we had not heard anything since I last talked to him. I wonder if I looked tired, out of place, and older to him. The devastation was here. It wasn't as visible, but he knew it was here.

I had felt as though everything I had said to try and console him the day of the

tornado was wrong or not helpful. Today, I felt as though he were trying to console me, but it just didn't make me feel any better. Maybe it was too close to somewhere I had already been.

————

At one point, after Dad had been there for a while, he and I were outside talking. He told me that the old man who lived up the street had said that he knew Jason had done it. I looked at him angrily and said, *"Done what?"* The old man, who lived about three houses away, had told Dad that he heard them fighting and hollering at each other a lot. I asked Dad if he remembered how Hollie and Jason talked to each other. They were loud people. They were *always* loud, always trying to talk over each other. I had talked to the old man the day before, and he told me he had seen Hollie that morning, but he also thought it was Thursday when it was Saturday. His family wouldn't let him out of the yard.

Dad and the others didn't stay but a few hours. I really didn't talk to them very much; it seems as though there were some cops there talking to us, or maybe Jan.

When they were leaving, Prentiss hugged me. I hadn't expected that. Then Sandra hugged me, and I almost fell apart. I knew that it would be hard for me if they were there and I was right. It was as though they were in a place I could no longer go. I thanked them for bringing up Dad.

I couldn't believe that everyone had forgotten so quickly what Hollie was like. No questions seemed to be about Hollie—just about Jason.

I talked to Dad later that night after they got home. He said someone there had asked him if we had checked out Jason before Hollie married him. That was not a good thing to ask Dad. What was he supposed to do? Go get a rope and hang Jason now to save everyone all the speculation?

Everyone there seemed to have a theory about what had happened. All of the theories involved either Jason or Hollie as a runaway. It is impossible to convey how cynical the attitudes were. It was as though no one knew her except Linda, Jason, Weslea, and me. The only thing we could do was look at each other and try to convince ourselves that all of this was part of a process that we had to endure in order to find Hollie.

The policemen asked very personal questions. I looked at the others in an effort to let them know that it was necessary.

I watched Jan's reports late that afternoon. I tried to eat something. Weslea was trying to get the media organized and was working with Hollie's friends and their distribution of the flyers. She seemed to have the capacity to stay focused. Martin left that afternoon to go home.

———

One day Hollie and I were coming from a subdivision called Northbay with a load of someone's discarded plants piled in the back of that old blue pickup. This was the first summer she worked with me in my landscaping business—it was maybe the first or second week into the summer.

We stopped at the red light in Madison and were behind an elderly couple in an old Ford pickup. (Hollie had on that big white cowboy hat of mine; her foot was on the dash, and she was talking to me and waving her hands as usual.) Anyway, the woman in front of us was wearing a big sun hat—every so often you could see her laugh while she was talking. They had a lawn mower in back. I said, "Hollie—now there's one thing you simply must understand if you work with me here in 'the city': that is—how we may be perceived as we go about our work." Then I pointed to the little old couple. Hollie looked at them and she said, "God, look at 'em— they look like us." Then she got tickled. I said, "They're shorter than us."

As they were turning away from us, the man leaned up and slapped the dash and started laughing. Hollie looked up at me and said, "I can deal with it."

———

Cops came by all day Sunday. When they would leave, all Jason would tell me was they were still asking about the time line, or trying to establish one. He was tiring of all the questions. All I could do was tell him it was part of the process, and that they had to learn as much as they could. He was withdrawn, which I thought was understandable. We were all very tired. He didn't talk much to anyone as the people came and went.

Diane got there that afternoon. The longer she was there, the more closed up Jason became. It is hard to describe how he was. Linda was very supportive of him. They had always gotten along really well. I'm sure Jason felt as though she was his only support.

Diane was impressed that all the people from GP had shown up. She would introduce them: "This is Jason's boss," or "He works at GP with Jason." I would think, "I don't care. *Do they know where Hollie is?*"

Weslea was busy, and seemed to be having a hard time helping Jason, as I was. But I couldn't help thinking that he would be O.K. He was alive, and we knew where he was. I figured anything else could be handled, even the questioning.

I can't really remember much else that happened during that day. I spent most of the time talking, either to the police, to friends of Hollie's and Jason's, or on the phone.

It seemed as though every time I walked through the house, Diane would say loudly, "When Hollie gets back," or "Hollie loves (this or that)." She had no idea she was being so hurtful. Diane was a very straightforward person and spoke exactly what was on her mind. Looking back, I can understand why Hollie liked her, but by the time she arrived Jason, Linda, and I had done very little talking to each other. Almost everything she said was something we were thinking but wouldn't say. Somebody asked her about driving all the way up, and she said she just had to come and touch Jason. Most of what she said was very easy to remember—*too easy, maybe.*

Night

I remember walking through their back yard Sunday night. They had fenced in part of it with wire for the puppies. I had given them the wire. They hauled it around in the Blazer for a couple of months before they put it up. They never did get it fixed right. It didn't keep the puppies in.

Jason had a retriever for which he had paid two hundred dollars. Hollie had decided she would go to the dog pound and get a puppy. She got some kind of sheep dog, a really big puppy with feet as big as dinner plates. I was walking around with them, and her puppy wanted to play. I kept walking off, and he kept following me around. I couldn't seem to make him go away. Hollie had brought him down to our house once, and he had followed her around. I knew he just wanted to play. Hollie would have played with him, but I couldn't handle it. I found myself sitting out on the curb, practically in the street behind their house, crying for the first time since I had gotten there. It must have been the puppy.

Linda came out to find me. I suppose I had been outside for a long time. When we went back inside people were standing around quietly looking at me. I guess I wasn't supposed to do that.

I kept telling Weslea to stay focused on finding Hollie. I was having a hard time with that myself. She seemed to have the capacity to keep going in one direction.

Sunday night at ten o'clock there was a police spokesperson on the news. He said there would be a news conference on Monday at twelve o'clock, and that they expected to have some new information about Hollie's case.

Everybody at the house got excited when they saw the report. The man looked like he knew what he was talking about.

After the news was over I took Linda outside and told her the only thing he could be talking about was Jason's polygraph test. I said, "Don't look forward to twelve o'clock tomorrow, because nothing will happen." I told her that I was sure if they knew anything about Hollie, they would have told us. *I was certain it was about Jason, not Hollie.*

It was a long, long day. I can't remember anything else about Sunday, which is good. *"Good night, Hollie—love ya."*

———

I think the best way to describe my feelings on that Sunday would be to use the word "responsible," strange though that may sound. I knew there was not any way I could change or control anything that was going on, but I felt as though everything I did or thought was in some way connected to Hollie. If I ate, I felt guilty, because I thought if Hollie were alive she would be hungry. I couldn't sleep—she might not be able to sleep. I couldn't relax—it wouldn't be right. I couldn't cuss—God might hear me and not give her back. I couldn't think Jason had anything to do with it, because what if she were an angel and she could see me? If he really didn't have anything to

do with it, she would surely be hurt that I had suspected him. Could an angel feel pain? If she were an angel, where was she? Was she with me? Was she so far away she would never be with me again? Why didn't I know any of these things? How was I supposed to? I would surely go to hell if I died now, because I didn't understand where angels were...

Maybe I would have understood if I had prayed more. Maybe I would not have understood anything—maybe God was punishing me. Maybe I was supposed to know everything. If she could see me, what if she was disappointed because I didn't know where she was? I didn't want her to be disappointed in me. I was afraid to say "God "—I might say it the wrong way. I could think of little else. What if she was alive, and they wouldn't let her go because I don't know how to talk to God?

———

Monday, April 14, 1997

Early Morning

Hollie had been gone for three nights and two days. We were all up early. Someone reminded me that I had been wearing the same shirt since I had gotten there. They got me some of Jason's clothes and told me I should take a shower.

I went with Jason to the police station so he could take the polygraph test. I had been talking to the police for two days now, and much of their questioning was about Jason. I felt I should be upset with them for even thinking about him, but I wasn't. I would have sacrificed myself or anyone else just to see her again. That in itself made me feel guilty about Jason. Hollie would want me to protect him *and* find her. I just couldn't seem to do either one— certainly not both.

Tom McCollum had told Jason the test would be given at eight-thirty. Jason, Diane, and I got to the police station a little after eight o'clock. I must have drunk a whole pot of coffee before we left the house.

They put us in a small waiting room with six straight-back chairs and a window with a hole in it for the receptionist to talk through. You couldn't see her when you were sitting. *All you could see were four gray walls.*

Diane had not stopped talking since she had arrived, and it seemed she never would. The only time I couldn't talk was while she was talking. This made me really mad.

We sat there until almost nine o'clock. Jason became more and more agitated; Diane talked faster and faster. The only thing I could do was to tell Jason, again, that it was just part of the process...

Tom came out about nine and told Jason that they were late getting set up, that we should go get some coffee and come back about nine-thirty. It did not take us long to find out that there were no coffee shops in downtown Texarkana.

When we got back we must have waited about forty-five minutes to an hour more before they came to get Jason.

Diane and I had been sitting there for about an hour when someone came out and told us they were having some trouble setting up the test. They said it would be about twelve o'clock before they would be finished. We left. I took Diane back to the house and got lost on the way. Diane said over and over, "They can't do Jason that way." She kept telling me where she and Hollie had gone on her visit there. We finally got to the house, and I dropped her off. I had to get away. No sleep, a lot of coffee, and Diane is not a good combination—anytime. We seemed to be trying to outtalk each other. I was simply no match for her. There was so much tension that I think we were all getting on each other's nerves.

I rode around by myself for about an hour. Then I went and picked her up, and we went back to the police department, getting there shortly before twelve o'clock. They told us it would still be a little while. I had to go outside for a walk. *I felt like I was coming unscrewed. I couldn't stay focused. I couldn't sit still. I was really having a hard time.* The idea that Jason might actually have had something to do with it was scaring the hell out of me. I had not considered this as a reality.

———

When Hollie and Weslea were teenagers we would send them on little church retreats in the summer. At some point during these meetings they would have some kind of prayer groups and ask the girls how they would like the others to pray for them. This was sort of a confession time for the kids there. They came from families with all sorts of problems— divorce, abuse, other difficulties.

Hollie and Weslea didn't really think they had any problems so they would just become very concerned about the other children. When they got home they would recount what the other ones had said, especially Weslea. She would always tell us what Hollie had said. When they would ask Hollie what her biggest fear was she would always tell them that it was losing her family, or part of her family, during her life. That never happened. I'm glad it never happened.

When I got back to the waiting room, Jason was still inside, and Diane was standing with Lt. Satterfield. He introduced himself and asked if I could come with him.

He was a big man. He looked like someone who had probably been a good football player at one time. He was very serious and very much in control of himself.

We went to his office. He told me he was in charge of the investigation and apologized for not having been there over the weekend, saying that he had been out of town.

I thought he must be in charge if he had the corner office. You could see all of Texarkana through the windows behind him. *He looked like another redneck in a suit to me.*

He leaned back in his chair and put the earpiece of his glasses against his front teeth. I had a banker who always did that. I thought, *"Maybe I can't do this. Maybe I can't talk. I really hate bureaucrats. He is in charge."* He said, "Mr. Calhoun, there are some things I can't talk about to fathers." I thought, *"Where do these people get their scripts? Same words. It has been three days. Same script."*

I talked to this man for two and a half to three hours. *I never cried.* I teared up once, and held the tears in my eyes the entire time.

I can't remember the sequence of the things that were said, but I will write as much as I can remember.

I told him that I knew Hollie was dead. I didn't care who killed her, but I intended for somebody in this damn place to find her. "There is not *anything* you can tell me that I haven't already thought of. *I know she is dead.*"

He asked me how I knew. I told him I had slept in her house Friday night—or at least I had lain in her bed. *I just knew she was dead.* He told me about a famous detective who would always lie in the victim's bed when he was working on a case. *Hollie—her name is Hollie—not "victim." Nobody can see Hollie. What am I going to do if nobody ever sees her again? She's not a runaway—she's Hollie. She is just Hollie...*

At some point, early in our conversation, he asked me what I thought about the police. I told him that so far the best detective he had was Jan, the TV person.

Me: "Did Jason pass the test?"

Satterfield: "No."

Me: "The test is not conclusive. I mean there are degrees or parts of it you can pass or fail—it is not concrete, right?"

Satterfield: "He failed it. There are no in-betweens. I watched part of it and I watched his interview on tape. There is no doubt in my mind that Jason loved Hollie. I think if he did kill her it was probably by accident or during an argument or something like that. I mean during sex. I'm sorry. If you had rather, I won't talk about it in that way."

Me: "I don't want you to keep telling me there are things you cannot tell me. They had been married six months. I realize they had sex. I never thought of it as fatal. Nothing will surprise me. My daughter is gone."

Satterfield: "I think they could have had an argument or maybe their sex had gotten a little out of control. Do you know if Hollie wore wigs? That wig is really hard to explain."

Me: "Not that I know of. I've never seen one."

He told me of a book he had read about a guy who kid-napped women and left strange items as clues. The odd assortment of objects that Jason had found reminded him of the book. What he had for evidence was a pack of cigarettes, a wig, and a missing telephone receiver. He thought Jason had placed them. He told me Jason's time-line was also a little off, but he never explained how.

After twenty-one years of life, Hollie had been reduced to a case number by a group of people who had never known her and never would. And they were my only hope of ever knowing what happened; without them I could never find her.

Me: "Let me tell you what I think about arresting Jason. I know this is a small town. I know GP basically runs things, and I know they want some results from you. I know the press is down your throat, and I do realize how easy it would be to hand Jason over to them. It's been three days. If you arrest him, your people will shut down, and the search for her will shut down, too. They will concentrate on Jason, not Hollie. You will never find her."

Satterfield: "I will keep detectives on the case until we find her."

Me: "There are people working everywhere to find her, her friends, people Jason works with—everybody is looking for Hollie. If Jason did have anything to do with it, we know she's gone, they will know that, too. If he did have something to do with it, how will we find her?"

Satterfield: "He will break—sooner or later, he will break. If I lock him up, he will break."

Me: "What if he doesn't break? What if he never breaks? What if he didn't do anything? Of all the things I don't know, the one thing I do know is that you cannot get hung up on him. He's the biggest target you have. He's here and he's easy."

Satterfield: "I don't have tunnel vision on this thing. I will keep our other leads working."

The police were continuously trying to establish a timeline. When they questioned Jason, they always told him that it was about the timeline.

What we knew of the timeline:

7:00 a.m.—Jason went to work.

7:30 a.m.—He attended a meeting at work.

12-12:30 p.m.—He checked his answer mail, and Hollie had called at 9:30. She told him he didn't have to call her back (she had called me at 9:38, but did not leave a message).

Jason said he tried to call her at lunch, but the phone was busy. He now assumed that was because the receiver was missing.

3:30 p.m.—Jason got home. Hollie was not there. He took a nap (I think for an hour or so). When he woke up he went to get pizza— two pizzas. When he got back he called her friends and asked if they had seen her.

8:00 p.m.—Linda called Jason

Me: "Like I told you—we have to find Hollie. I'm not trying to close a case—just find Hollie."

Satterfield: "What kind of relationship did you and Hollie have?"

Me: "When I thought sometimes about dying I would wonder who Hollie would talk to if I was gone, and I would worry about whether she could talk with someone else the way she does with me. She uses me as a sounding board and I kind of like that— it keeps me in touch. I was trying to stay out of their business, but Hollie liked to talk to me sometimes. Maybe she talked for me, but that doesn't matter. I probably knew her as well as any one, other than Jason."

Satterfield: "What do you think she would do if someone pulled a gun on her?"

Me: "I think she would try to determine what she would have to do to survive. I don't think she would run through the house screaming. Maybe that's not good, but I think she would try and deal with it. I think she would do what the person told her to do to buy herself some time. I always told her not to panic; it would get her hurt." (Now, I think that the only way she might have survived would have been if she had panicked.)

November 10, 1997

Monday, April 14, 1997, Continued

Satterfield: "Can you describe Hollie—her personality? What's she like? I've seen her pictures; I know she smiles a lot."

Me: (I had been asked this so many times over the last few days, and since I had not been able to do that—describe her—maybe it was more critical than I had thought. *No one knew her.*) "Hollie was a good kid. I spanked her once or twice when she was little. I learned very early that I could not force her to do things if she thought she was right. I would have to talk to her even when she was small. She always had a logical reason for doing what she did—at least it was logical to her. She was determined. She was *strong willed*. She looked up to her sister, who is very religious, and

Weslea kind of kept Hollie straight, you know. I
went broke farming in the eighties, and after
Hollie was older I felt as though she could relate
more to the money situation than her sister or her
mom could. What I'm saying is, she was not naive
about those things. She kept their bills paid. She
helped me with my landscaping business the last
couple of summers. She's not weak *physically*."

Satterfield: "I have a daughter; Hollie sounds like her."

As he talked he was looking over my shoulder at the
bookcase behind me—pictures of his family were placed
across the top. He leaned back and looked at those pictures for what seemed like a very long time. I never
turned around and looked at the pictures. *I looked at him.*
When he looked back at me he didn't say anything at
first, but I knew he had *seen* Hollie. I just knew. After
three days somebody had finally seen Hollie. I thought,
*"Thank you, God—he saw her. She does look like your
daughter. She could be your daughter. She could be anyone's
daughter. She's not a runaway. She's not on dope. She loves her
family just like your daughter does. She is a good person just
like your daughter is, and I love her just like you love your
daughter. You have to feel that—you have to feel the pain. We
have to find her..."*

Satterfield: "We don't have any unsolved murder cases
here. I will find Hollie."

Me: "I will do anything—anything. I just don't know
what to do."

Satterfield: "You keep your family together."

Me: "What am I supposed to do with Jason? How do I deal with him?"

Satterfield: "You don't do anything. We'll handle it."

He shook my hand and told me I could call him any time. He said he would stay in touch with me, and he promised me again that he would find Hollie. He was concentrating on Jason. There was not much I could do about that now. He was the only person I had talked to since we had gotten there who told me that we would find Hollie. When I walked out of his office, Weslea, Jason, Diane, and Gary Maye were waiting for me.

I'm not sure exactly how long they had been waiting, but Weslea seemed very glad to see me. I was glad to see Gary, who had been Weslea's pastor when she lived in Jackson. I felt as though he would be a lot of help for Weslea.

Gary was surely sent to us. Weslea had asked if she should call him Sunday.

Weslea told me later that I seemed to be in a very good mood when I walked out. I think that may have confused her a little. I had been in there for two hours. There would never be a way for me to explain to her how happy I was that somebody had actually seen Hollie as a real person.

Weslea told me she thought maybe I had fallen apart, judging from how screwed up I had seemed when I left the house earlier. *Maybe that is why she was there. She must have been concerned about me. I was not aware that anyone knew how messed up I was. Amazing.*

It was almost dark when we got back to the house. We

all ate supper together that night, or at least we all sat down at the same time. There was enough food for fifty people. I had some kind of rice dish with chicken on top of it. I ate almost all of the rice and no meat. They all made fun of me for eating so much rice. No one else could eat it. I really couldn't remember when I had eaten last.

Gary was like a relief valve on a pressure cooker. He is easy with people and very cool. Walking into a situation like ours and finding a way to make everyone relax is certainly a gift. It was the first laughter that had been heard in a long time.

He had brought all the suits he owned or at least all that the trunk of his car would hold. I knew he was committed; that was most important to me. He said he didn't know how long he would have to stay or what he would need to do, but he wanted to be well dressed. He was Weslea's salvation. She worried about me and Linda, and I was worried about her. She was so focused—so intense.

Weslea and Gary were quite good with the media, and, because of them and Jan, Hollie's picture was on TV almost every newscast.

Night

Linda, Weslea, and I stayed in a motel Monday night. We pushed the beds together and slept on one big bed, wanting to be close. We went to sleep about twelve or one o'clock. At 2:38 we all awoke, sat up in the bed, and looked at each other. Nobody had said anything, but we all woke up at the same time. It must have been some kind of negative energy or something.

Tuesday, April 15, 1997

Early Morning

Linda, Weslea, and I got up at about five o'clock on Tuesday. Someone had said we might want to check the airport, and Wes wanted to take some of the flyers over there first thing. She and Gary would return and go through all the old warehouses at the airport. Weslea found a woman there who let her in and helped her look for Hollie. The woman's own sister had been kidnapped and later found. Weslea told me that Gary would stand in the door, and she would go through and look for Hollie, *calling for her sister.*

I don't believe I could have done it, but Weslea was so determined. I think it still scares her when she realizes what she did.

After we had gone to the airport and I had taken Weslea and Linda back to Hollie's house, I went to get Gary at the motel. He had stayed in the room next to ours Monday night. I wanted to talk to him alone. I had been thinking about Jason since I talked to the lieutenant. I was really beginning to think about him hurting Hollie. It was very hard not to do that after the last couple of days.

On our way back to the house, I just drove around for a while and talked to Gary. I suppose that it only proved my weakness spiritually, but there were some things I could not seem to stop thinking about. I needed to ask him some questions. If Hollie were dead and truly an angel—could she see me? Could she hear me? Did she know when I thought about Jason? Did it hurt her? Could she feel pain if she were an angel? Gary never answered me. I knew he didn't know. Maybe I scared him. Maybe I didn't shut up long enough to let him answer.

After we talked I decided it didn't matter. Hollie would expect me to do what I could to find her. I think she would have understood if I were to have to sacrifice Jason's feelings or trust.

The more the police focused on Jason and the worse he looked, the closer Linda got to him.

Night

Tuesday night was a little different. We were at Hollie's, and it must have been ten or eleven o'clock when Jason realized there were some other things missing. Until this point the only object we thought was missing was the receiver off the phone. Then Jason noticed that his brief-case, which had a very expensive calculator in it, was gone. Diane, who had bought the briefcase, kept telling us how much it had cost. Next, Jason couldn't find their tent (who would steal a tent?), and some items that went with the tent were also gone. I asked him if there was anything else. Jason started walking through the house. This was the first time he had been in their bedroom. *I didn't know that.* Diane took a legal pad and followed him around. When he would name something she would write it down, and then she would say, "They can trace that— that's worth [such and such]; it's easy to sell." A glass full of pennies was missing from their dresser. *Who steals pennies?* It was now about one or two Wednesday morning. Somebody finally said we should call the FBI agent, Tom McCollum, and Jason did. Diane stood beside him as he spoke into the phone. Jason would name an item on the list, and Diane would tell him to describe it and say how much it had cost. They were both talking at the same time—Jason to Tom, Diane to Jason. After about five or ten minutes of this, Tom asked Jason to give the phone to Diane. I was so glad. This was the strangest thing I had ever seen. It was the fifth day, not the first. I couldn't help thinking, "How could you *not* miss a tent, for God's sake, or a brief-case, and who steals pennies?" *This seemed so wrong.* It just didn't set right. Maybe it was Diane's loud-speaker voice. *This was beginning to really, really bother me.* How could someone have been in the house for so long, and why would they take so many strange little things of almost no value and leave the place so clean? *How could Hollie be gone?* After so many days, how could no one here know anything about what happened?

It didn't matter whether or not the items were traceable. *Absolutely nothing fit together—not anything—not even as a crime scene.* It looked as though Hollie had just put some things together and walked out. Since I am not a police-man, I didn't know that sometimes a place being clean to this extent indicated that something criminal had hap-pened there. *It was too clean.*

I had to get out of there—quickly. I couldn't listen to this any-more. When Diane finally finished screaming at Tom and got off the phone, I told Jason that we were going to leave now and give him a chance to concentrate on what else might be missing. *That was all I could say. I could hardly talk.* I felt as though I had stepped into some kind of vacuum. Maybe I was just exhausted. The others didn't seem as bothered by the whole scene as I was. Everybody kept say-ing, "They can trace that—it will be easy." The sleeping bags were gone. Hollie's makeup was not gone.

November 15, 1997

Hollie was alive eight months ago. Hollie was alive. Then I was working and not thinking much about anything important, like life and death. I have changed to some extent. I think I made it cost too much, in the ways I have used people to cushion the pain that was so intense in the early summer. I cannot believe some of the things that I did and how I let people help me so much. I have always had a problem asking for help, but I began to expect it. At some point, I will have to try to make amends.

I found it very hard to be productive or even just to keep going, without help. It's hard to admit that you are much weaker than you ever wanted to be. Weslea would tell me I need to go to church more often, and maybe she is right. Judi would tell me I had not taken advantage of anyone, and that I am not weak. Hollie would tell me it was about time to get it together and move on. I will have to make an adjustment.

April 15, 1997, Continued

Night

What kind of a person steals pennies and sleeping bags?

I f Hollie's makeup had been gone I would have thought she had just packed up and left, but every-thing missing was related to camping, except that expensive briefcase. *Five days had passed.* We had been in the house a lot. This was just too strange. I couldn't tell anyone how I felt. Finally, I decided something might be wrong with me, and that this might, after all, be a good turn of events. All of the items *would* be easy to trace. *This just might be a good thing.*

I slept very little that night. I kept thinking about the objects that were missing. They had to be the strangest clues ever. *This all seemed to be so wrong.*

The house was so clean. Nothing was turned over or broken, and nothing was out of place. Some things were missing, and *Hollie was gone.*

(I know there is something in here—
there has to be something. I am growing
tired writing this. This is only stuff. Hollie
is not in here. She was not even a partici-
pant. Everything that happened after the
first day was just stuff; she was gone. I cannot seem to get past the "event," as everyone called it. I did for awhile. Maybe I try
to write too much at one time, but I just
can't stop thinking about writing it down.
It is almost as if I want it to hurt some more.

When I started writing this I thought it
would help me to get through before I
have to go back for the trial. I really don't
want to go back. I will have to get past all
of this writing and pain—quickly. The way
I feel is not a good thing.)

———

By Tuesday I had talked to Kim a good deal. She was
becoming more and more concerned about Dad. I probably told her more about what I knew than I did anyone
else. Mother had her whole family around her—her sister,
brother, and others. Dad had gathered the people of
Puckett around him, but most of them had to go back to
work on Monday, so he was at home with Mother's family
and the friends who came by. He would not leave the
house. Kim and I decided it would be better for Mother
not to come. She seemed to be doing O.K. as long as she
had family and friends around her. We had decided that

Kim should fly down Tuesday because Dad wanted to come back to Arkansas on Wednesday. Kim was to fly down, pick him up, and bring him to Texarkana. Kim and her husband, Sam, had decided that the person involved in Hollie's disappearance must be someone who was very clever and very much a criminal. The only problem they saw was the cigarettes, which were the cheapest brand you could buy. Kim said that meant that the person smoked a lot but could not afford to, like somebody on dope or a kid. *Maybe somebody planted them.* They had been on the table in the kitchen, and only one was missing. (As it turned out, Kim's first thought was right. It was dope. I mean, the person was a dope-head and a real criminal.)

We decided that if somebody had planted the cigarettes there, it meant that they had planned to take Hollie. We were not prepared to think about that kind of criminal being in her house. The police had found no fingerprints on the pack.

Linda's theory was that a gang had taken Hollie. She would watch the news and was very vocal about how we would find Hollie.

Weslea and Gary continued to work with Hollie's friends and with the press. They were very busy.

Linda was getting closer and closer to Jason. It was a mother thing, I suppose. Jason would tell her every morning that today would be the day we would get Hollie back. Linda, the way I saw it, was carrying him to some extent. When Linda and I talked we didn't talk about finding Hollie or getting her back. We would talk about Weslea and other people. Actually, I can't remember a lot of what we *did* talk about. Linda had spoken to her parents maybe two or three times since Saturday, falling apart when she did. Her mother had called me on Monday and asked if they could come Wednesday. They wanted to touch Linda. Everybody wanted to touch their children.

Wednesday, April 16, 1997

Wednesday was a very, very, long day. We moved to the Georgia Pacific guest house. Dad and Kim were coming up, and Linda's parents were due. This was the sixth day. *There was very little hope for Hollie. I could not imagine her surviving anything for this long. (I cannot see any good coming from this. It has become too much of an obsession for me to write. There is no net here.)*

We all went to Hollie's early in the morning. We were getting the phones forwarded and putting other things in order so that we could leave the house. Everybody else left for the GP house; I was to stay until Kim and Linda's parents arrived. It was hard to wait for the others to leave, but I wanted to call Lt. Satterfield and needed to be alone when I did.

I called him early. I asked him if he had seen the list of

missing items that Jason had given to Tom. He said he had gone over it earlier with Tom.

Me: "This is a good thing, right? I mean, there are some things on there that can be pawned and traced."

Satterfield: "Some of the things might be easy to find if they are pawned. I have a woman sitting in front of a computer that is tied to every pawn shop in the country. That is all she will do."

Me: "This is beginning to look more like a robbery or like maybe somebody else is involved. That was a lot of stuff, don't you think?"

Satterfield: "Now don't get me wrong, I don't have tunnel vision. We are checking out all these things, but my opinion has not changed."

Me: "How could Jason have had anything to do with that stuff? He couldn't have taken it out after Saturday. You have a thousand pictures of the house taken Saturday. Those things would have to have been taken out before then. He wouldn't have been stupid enough to do that after the pictures."

Satterfield: "He could have taken them out before the pictures."

Me: "The only way he could have done that would be if he had planned to hurt Hollie. That makes no sense. That doesn't add up. How could that work, and why? Why would anybody do that? If he did that, why would he wait five days?"

Satterfield: "I don't know that yet. There are so many
   things that just don't add up. Why don't I come by
   and we can talk. I'll be there in about an hour."

After we hung up I decided that maybe he didn't want
to talk because the phones were tapped. And then I decided it must be something very serious. It must be about
Jason. *It couldn't be good.*
   The clothes I had on didn't fit me. Dad had brought me
some clothes on Sunday, but the pants were too big, the
shirt was too small, and the shoes didn't look right. *I need
to find some more shoes. This is so uncomfortable. I wonder why
I decided to stay here alone. There is nobody to call right now.
There are so many pictures. There must be twenty pictures in
here. No wonder they didn't have any money; they bought too
many picture frames. It is quiet in here. So many pictures.
Maybe I should go for a walk. Maybe I should get out of the
house. I can't leave. It's so quiet. It's too quiet—much too quiet.
I have to stay here—people are coming. This is the first time I
haven't had somebody around to talk to. I know they don't listen—it doesn't matter. I have to move around and talk. It feels so
strange in here—as if Hollie were here, but not comfortable like
the time we visited—just strange.*
   *Did you think we would forget that you were married? Did
you have to frame all these pictures? And who frames pictures of
puppies? What's that about anyway? I'm in almost all the pictures. I didn't want to be in these pictures. My god, my hands
are in all the pictures. I didn't want to give you away, I didn't
want to lose you. I didn't know.*
   *Do you hear me, damn it? I know you can hear me. I can feel
you, I know you're here. Why is the ceiling so low?*

Why didn't you tell me? We talked so long last Saturday night. I felt that there was something wrong. What did you think I would do if you told me? Why didn't you tell me? Why?

Talk to me! I can feel you here. I know you are here. I want to know why you didn't tell me! You told me everything.

If you are not going to talk to me, then don't get this close! I can't see anything but my damn hands. Giving you up—I wouldn't have given you up. You know that! Can you hear me? I know you can hear me.

This was a really long conversation, and it went downhill from there. I don't remember exactly what I said.

I can cry. If I cry I will feel better—just a little. People are coming. I can't cry long.

Thirty minutes later I was sitting in the bathroom crying into a huge towel. I really didn't think I would ever stop. *I thought that I would die there. It hurt so much.* Crying was making me cry. I couldn't seem to stop. I had never felt anything like that before. All those pictures and *my* hands. *I gave her up.* What if I had given her up to somebody who killed her? What if she had trusted me, and I had given her up to somebody who killed her?

I heard a car door outside. It was probably either the lieutenant or Dad.

One of the strangest feelings I've ever had was when I stopped crying. *I just stopped, got off the floor, and wiped my face. I was O.K.* People were here. *Hollie was gone.* There were no feelings inside me. It was Dad and Kim. I was glad to see them. Kim had come a long way. They came in, and, while I talked to Dad, Kim just looked around. She had never been to Hollie's house, and I think it was hard on her being there, although I never asked her. We had

talked so much about where things were in the house, and
I think actually seeing it all set her back some. A few minutes later the lieutenant got there. I asked Dad and Kim if
they would ride around for a little while so I could talk to
him alone. They left, and the lieutenant and I went into the
living room. It looked kind of strange in there, because I
had thrown everything around (mostly pillows and chairs,
nothing that would break) during the conversation I had
had with Hollie in my mind.

Me: "What couldn't you tell me on the phone?"

Satterfield: "There are just some things that we have
            turned up that lead me to believe that Jason had
            something to do with it. And I *don't* have tunnel
            vision. We are getting so many leads. We have
            even gotten some leads from St. Louis, but what
            we have doesn't help Jason."

Me: "What?" He leaned back and didn't say anything
      for a few minutes. We just looked at each other.
      "You can't *not* tell me. What is it?"

The conversation that followed was without a doubt the
most intense one Satterfield and I had had. His attitude
toward me and his manner of dealing with the case had
been direct and professional until now, but new evidence
had been uncovered, and he felt he was getting closer to
finding some answers. His demeanor changed. Suddenly
we were in this together. He began to draw me into his
playing field, disclosing new information that centered the
blame more and more on Jason. Satterfield was cautious

about what he told me, but I could feel his intensity growing stronger as he talked, and we began to communicate on a different level. Jason had been drilled over and over about his timeline, and Satterfield's conversations with people from GP, neighbors, and two new witnesses revealed inconsistencies in Jason's story. The fact that Jason had given the first account on the evening of Hollie's disappearance possibly explained why it wasn't completely accurate. His emotional and psychological state was less than fine at the time, but the FBI and police wanted to either prove or disapprove Jason's story, and so far they were developing a mercilessly strong case against him. There was a moment during this conversation when I fully understood what a devastating position Jason was in. The only thing I can remember after that moment was that the lieutenant looked as mad as I felt. About halfway through our conversation, he got a page. He returned the call and found that it was his daughter, who couldn't get his lawn mower started. He talked to her for a little while and kept trying to get off the phone. I just sat there and looked at him. I never said anything, and he didn't say anything about her when he finally got off. *I guess his daughter was something like my girls.* I never acknowledged his daughter. I regret that a little, now; it never crossed my mind at the time.

I told him at some point that he had become too emotionally involved, and I didn't see how he could get so close to these kinds of cases on a regular basis. He told me he never had, until this one. He said it was not his nature.

When I think about it now, I really do believe he was trying to prepare me for one of the most painful moments possible in a person's life. He had seen these situations before and knew that the people involved would be just about at their limit of coping. I know I wasn't dealing with events very well. I had already felt the pain of thinking that Jason might have hurt her.

We must have talked for about an hour. It was very intense, as it had been on Monday. I was speaking more honestly, or at least I thought I was. As the lieutenant left I asked him to please call me before they arrested Jason so I could get Linda and Weslea away from the house.

When he left, Dad and Kim were back and waiting for me in the front yard. I don't know what time it was. Sam and Nell (Linda's parents) had gotten there and were waiting with Kim and Dad. After the lieutenant left, Dad, Sam, and Nell went to the GP house.

Kim and I took Jason's Blazer, and I said we would be back in a little while.

When we were by ourselves I told Kim everything I knew, which was nothing, really, but at the time it felt like everything. *It was so heavy.* I was telling her too much; she had just gotten there, and I knew this was not fair. She had been trying to put things together from seven hundred miles away and reminded me of myself. She was suspicious of everyone in Texarkana, except me. It was impossible to stand in Hollie's house and not be shaken. We had talked so much about what might have happened, and what I was telling her did not help her cope with the situation any better. But I had to tell somebody, and it seemed to help at the time just to have someone to talk to who wouldn't fall apart. I guess I thought that if Kim did fall apart, I could put her back together. That was a lot for me to assume.

We must have ridden around for a few hours. Then I couldn't find the GP house, and by the time we got there it was almost dark. Gary was cooking for everybody. He liked to cook, and it seemed to ease the tension just for him to be doing something for everyone. Before we had gotten there, Kim had asked me what I did when I was around Jason, how I was handling it. She asked what she was supposed to do. I said, "Do what I do. Nobody knows anything for sure right now, and you have to assume that he had nothing to do with it. Stay close to me. I've had a couple of days to work on it, so just watch me—you will be O.K.

"You have to understand that if Jason did do anything, he is the only one who knows where she is. I don't know how to make him tell us. The police do know, or at least that is what I'm betting on right now. Just remember that there is a possibility he was involved. I know it is hard to deal with. You will need to give Diane a lot of room because she is extremely hard to take. She will make you mad just talking about the weather."

Diane and Jason would leave from time to time, and for some reason this made the situation even worse. Anyway, we finally got to the house, and after we had been there for a while I think Kim began to relax a little.

Jason was trying to fish in the lake that was behind the house. I was standing outside and Dad came over and said, "How can he just be standing there fishing? It doesn't look good for him to do that." I said that maybe it didn't look too good for us to be watching him fish either. He went on to tell me that Linda was going to have to accept the fact that Hollie might not be coming back, and that he had said so to her. I said, "We have been here for five days, and Linda and I will accept that when we are ready, or when they find Hollie. You know Linda and me well enough to know that we are not so stupid as not to realize Hollie may be dead, but you cannot force us to accept that unless we know for sure—and we don't."

While I was talking to him, Sam was talking to Linda. It seems that he had driven up there to tell Linda that she was going to have to accept the fact that Hollie was dead, and that she would have to go on with her life.

Linda and I decided it might be a good time to go for a walk. I guess that was the only time we both had cried any together, and I didn't cry much. She looked at me and asked me what we were going to do if Hollie didn't come back. *She cried.* I guess the others had thought they were doing the right thing in talking to us as they had.

We were gone for a little while. When we came back Gary had supper ready and everybody seemed to be a little better—or at least they were trying to be. Dad and Sam talked for a long time by themselves. I thought this might be what they both needed.

Weslea and I both talked to Tom McCollum at some point that night. Tom was now trying to convince us that this was going to take a long time. Every time somebody talked to him, that was his main topic. I guess he must have known it would be hard for us just to stay there and wait. Our entire family was there or had gone back and forth more than once. We had stayed at the GP house, motels, and Hollie's house. We were of no help to the police; we just simply could not leave. Everyone in the family who was there, I believe, thought that Hollie was close—*we could not leave.* Tom had been here before and understood how hard it was for everyone to be away from home and waiting. We understood what he was trying to tell us, but it was almost impossible for us to accept.

A TV crew from one of the local stations came over after supper. They did an interview with Jason, and they took some shots of Linda and me walking around the lake. Weslea was becoming more and more depressed about Jason. She couldn't get him to help her with anything. She would tell him where to be and what to do, trying to work closely with him, mostly to get ready for the interviews. It seemed to be what was keeping her going. They were reacting in totally different ways, but Weslea's intensity and timing which were required to put together those TV spots, and Jason's ability to simply program himself and say the necessary words at the appropriate time came together well on TV.

It must have been about two or three o'clock Thursday morning before Kim and I had another chance to talk. I thought everyone else had gone to bed when Weslea came in and sat down with us.

Weslea told us about her conversations with Tom and with the private detective I had talked to when we had first got there. She asked if we had talked to anyone, or if we knew anything she had not heard. Then I began to relate some of the things that the police had been telling me. I felt it was time for her to know that they were going to arrest Jason. She had already realized they were very close to arresting him and told us some things that I had not con-sidered. She and I were both very matter-of-fact about what we were saying. She had much more to say than I did. She was sitting on the sofa with Kim, and I was sitting across from them. When Wes would say something so absolute and so intense Kim would just look at me. Then she would tear up a little, get up and walk around the sofa, and sit down again. Wes would continue our conversation. Kim had been up since five o'clock Wednesday morning, had driven for seven hours with Dad, had listened to me for three or four hours as we rode around in that old Blazer, and had eaten supper with the only suspect that the police seemed to have. Now she was trying to deal with this: her little niece talking about Hollie's kidnapping or murder or whatever it might turn out to be. I can't imagine what shape she was in emotionally and physically.

Weslea was sitting on the edge of the sofa with her hands in her lap and her back straight; she was talking in a very direct manner to Kim and me. I was so tired that I could not have shown any emotion about what was being said, and I contributed little to the conversation.

———

As I watched and listened to Weslea I remembered a time when she was three or four years old. We had moved to the country from an apartment in the city. Wes was having a little trouble adjusting to all the woods around our house, and had decided that bears were out there. We could hardly get her out of the house to play. I realized after this had gone on for a while that she was not going to get past it by herself.

One day, I told her to hold my hand,

saying that we were going for a little walk. As we went through the yard and into the woods she squeezed my hand so tightly that the ends of her little fingers turned white, but she walked with me anyway. I knew that if she held onto my hand long enough she would realize there was no danger in the woods.

As we walked, we began to see some small animals and birds, and she started talking a little. She relaxed her grip. Then we came across some wildflowers. "Mom would love these, wouldn't she, Dad?" She let go of my hand and picked her mom some of those little flowers. I don't remember having another conversation with her about the bears.

Now, as I watched her sitting on the sofa and talking with so much confidence in her voice during this terrible time, I wanted so much to say, "Would you please let me hold your hand? I want to go home now. I am so very afraid here, because I know for certain—there is no doubt in my mind—that there are bears in *these* woods."

After all, we were talking about her brother-in-law being arrested for killing her sister. This was, to say the least, a hard subject to talk about with anyone. I can't begin to explain how hard it was to talk to *her* about it. *She wanted to know everything.* Surprisingly, she was satisfied with very little information. She just wanted us to know that she was going to participate, and that was much easier for me, actually.

We must have talked for a couple of hours. We were honest and direct with each other. When Wes would ask me something or tell me something about Hollie, Kim would sometimes just look at me and tear up; at other times she would get up and walk around the room. It was hard for her to add to the conversation, because we had been there for so long and she had been there for such a short time. She hadn't been talking to the police for five days as we had. This was a cruel way for her to have to deal with the situation. I know the day had been as long for her as it had been for me. By three o'clock that morning we had exhausted all of what we thought were our options regarding what we were going to do from this point on.

We had little hope by now that this was going to end quickly. We thought we should begin to get ourselves ready to go home, at least for a little while. Every time we talked to Tom he would tell us that these kinds of cases always took a long time. We talked to him often; I supposed he would be glad to see us leave—even for a little while.

Wes and I knew it would take a while to convince Linda that we should go. She would not want to leave Jason there without support.

We decided that we would leave on Friday. Thursday, we would get ready to go.

Thursday, April 17, 1997

I don't remember much about Thursday. Dad and Linda's parents went home early that morning. Gary left in the afternoon. I really missed Gary; he had kind of held everything together.

A lot of store owners in Texarkana had put signs on their storefronts that said *Hope for Hollie*. Kim and I put the lettering on a couple of those portable signs. That was hard to do. *I had very little hope.*

The only other thing I remember is being in one of the offices in the GP house with Weslea at about eleven o'clock that night. She was sitting at the desk talking with Tom on the phone. She looked as though she were running a small business, just taking care of that day's details. He must have asked her about going into Hollie's house that night to pick up something. She told him to just go on in because the house was unlocked. He must have said something like, "Why would you leave it unlocked? Nobody is there." She said, "There is nothing of any value there, and if somebody gets everything—it doesn't matter. If Hollie comes back home, we left this phone number for her. We want her to be able to get into her house and call us if she can." She was so matter-of-fact about it. *The scene was unreal.* Tom didn't ask her anything else about the house.

I just sat there looking at her, hoping she would stay on the phone for a few more minutes, because that would at least give me time to breathe, and maybe I could talk when she hung up. Without a little time I could not have said a word. When she did hang up, we continued our conversation—*about what, I don't know.*

December 2, 1997

If I were an artist I would paint a picture.
In the center there would be a wall
reaching from the bottom to the top. Even
though the wall has taken very little space
you would know that it is infinite—
there is no bottom and there is no top.

If I were an artist the wall would be
the first thing you would see when you
looked at my painting, and you would
feel its impregnability.

At the very top on the right side of the
wall, you would see God facing away
from the wall. His arms are outstretched;
his hands are together with the palms up.
And lying in the palms of his hands, there
is an angel—sleeping—and God is pleased.

On the left side of the wall at the
very bottom there is a tiny little man
sitting with his back against the wall,
his legs drawn against his body, his arms
crossed on his knees, and his head bowed
on his arms.

If I were an artist you would see as I see.

Friday, April 18, 1997

On Friday, we left. I went by Hollie's that morning. Nobody wanted to leave except me. Not even Kim. I don't think I could have made it without her that morning. All I could say was, "It's time to go." Weslea was having an extremely hard time leaving the house. I think she felt as if she had failed Hollie completely by just walking away.

Kim talked a lot on the way home about her boys and other matters. It was good to have some different topics of conversation, and I was grateful to her.

Wes and Linda cried a little from time to time, but the situation seemed to get slightly better after we had been gone for a while.

When we got home I told somebody that I felt like I had pulled the car there with a chain. *It was a long ride.*

———

*That was the end of
the first 186 hours.*

———

What if:

I were an old man; would I sit on my porch and wonder why? Or would I sit on my porch killing ants with a walking stick, talking about people who lived early in my life, and wondering why I'm sitting here on my porch talking to someone I love, but who can never understand me?

Would I wonder if he would ever understand me? How could he, when there are so many years between us?

There are too many days—too many births—too many deaths. How would I make him understand, give him some way to cushion his pain? Maybe I would sit and talk about things that happened long ago. Maybe he would understand if he could see my life—if he could see the changes in my life, all the joy, all the losses, everything that has made me see clearly.

What if I could make him see more clearly without his living out all the days—without all the losses in his life, would he be a better person? Would he be the same person?

Maybe we aren't supposed to see more clearly...

PART THREE

The Second Week

December 14, 1997

W hen I started writing this I thought I was looking
for something—maybe strength or closure of some
kind. There is no closure. What I was looking for
is not here. The writing has become something of an obsession. I need to finish it. I need to finish it.

The Week of Saturday, April 19, 1997

It felt as though getting home took days, and when we
finally did arrive, I had the strangest feeling about being
here. Reality seemed to have been stolen from the house.
Everything was just as we had left it exactly a week earlier, but nothing appeared to be in the right place. The
plants in my pickup that I had bought for someone had
almost all wilted and died. I felt as though I couldn't

touch anything. It was as if everything here had been frozen in time the night we left. Imagine being taken back to something terrible that happened in your past and being made to stand there in the minute before it happened; only this time you realize it is going to happen, and you know you can't stop it. You just have to be there in that last minute.

We had two puppies of our own at that time—*and the puppy Hollie had given me.* They had all been fed well, but even they seemed displaced—*and that puppy—that damn puppy was so happy to see us.* I had been keeping her with me most of the time, and I suppose she had had an unpleasant week, too. The other two dogs were full grown and were sometimes mean to her.

I was on the phone a lot that week. People realized that we were home and would call and tell us that they were praying for us. We heard from many good people, but I always felt like saying that we had prayed almost nonstop for a week and the only thing I could figure out was that we and God didn't seem to be in the same time frame.

I would sit on our patio, talking to people, staring at the flower beds that Hollie had helped her mom fix last summer, and looking at the potted ferns Linda had placed on the steps. At Hollie's a couple of months earlier, Hollie and I were standing on the steps in front of her house and she was showing me what a good job she had done of cleaning the flower beds around the front porch. She pointed at some ferns and said that she wasn't sure what they were but that she liked them. I told her they were "Holly ferns." She smiled as though someone had named them after her and asked if I wanted to dig some up and take them home.

I told her there was no reason to and that we had to go. Linda and Jason came out, and Hollie went around behind the house. We were walking to the car, and she came back with a shovel and handed it to me, along with a couple of bags for the ferns. She just smiled—so I brought the ferns and the puppy home. (This is the puppy that I mentioned earlier, saying that I could not bear to bury it, too.)

When we were in Texarkana I would watch the police and the FBI and everybody step over, jump over, and walk around those beds, and I don't think anyone ever stepped on one of the ferns. Why would God take such good care of those plants and give Hollie up? I miss Hollie a lot and cannot believe that another human being killed her. I have not let myself think of it for so long that I believe I am going to have a very hard time for a little while. I cannot describe how unreal it seems that one person decided to take her away and that all this pain is the result of what he did. I can hardly think about anything except I don't understand why in these cases they don't let the victim's father kill the murderer. I really do think that I would take the chance of dying and going to hell if I could kill him. If that is what it's all about I really don't care anyway. It would be worth whatever it took to watch him die. I can do nothing—and people tell me that I seem to be O.K. and that good things come from tragedies like this. We all know that is BS and that nothing I do or write is going to change the situation. There will never be enough words to express how I feel about this SOB—there will never be Hollie again. I've thought and written so much about nothing, and I won't ever understand why he just sits there—there is no trade. She won't reappear when he dies, if he does get the death penalty. I think we are programmed to accept this sort of nightmare; over time, they say, you can get used to anything. Weslea says you can't dwell in sin. I can't stay on this page or I will lose my mind. There has to be a way to reach some sort of peace about this. I know I won't have the opportunity to kill him. I know I can't stay there. I know I have to pray. I don't know how to pray. I really don't feel much anymore—I'm not sure I ever did. I don't think I have changed. Well, good night, sweetie, I really do think that you and God are going to have to get together and help me through this for a short while.

The Saturday after we got back Kim went home. Weslea stayed for the weekend.

One thing I remember about the trip home that Friday is that I was beginning to feel the way many others did—*I had given up completely, now.* I was worried about Linda and Weslea, especially Linda, because she was still very much holding on to some hope that Hollie was alive and that Jason was not involved. I was so concerned by now that the police were going to arrest him that I couldn't function very well. I couldn't seem to make Linda understand this possibility, but at the same time I had never sat her down and told her, or even Wes, *everything* the police had told me. I thought that when I did they would immediately feel like I had on Wednesday morning. I didn't realize at the time that they could not feel like I felt unless they believed what I believed. *I only knew that nobody should have to feel that way without some help from somewhere, or at least somebody around them for a little support.*

I had talked to Brother Alvin quite a bit while we were in Arkansas. He had been Weslea and Hollie's pastor when they were young. So when I decided that it would be necessary to sit everyone down and explain the situation about Jason, I thought it would be good to have Brother

Alvin there. The pain that I had put myself through the past Wednesday morning thinking that Jason had possibly done something to Hollie was *always* part of what I was thinking. I worried that the same would be true for them if they knew, and I guess I thought Brother Alvin could pick up the pieces.

After I had taken Kim to the airport Saturday, I went on to see Brother Alvin. (Kim and I were late for the plane because we were eating fried chicken and talking. We promised we wouldn't tell anybody.)

Brother Alvin baptized both Weslea and Hollie. If Hollie was in Heaven at this point I truly did believe, and still believe, she is there because of him. After he went through the last few weeks with us and with as much as I had told him, I think that he knew I believed that. He has always been very important to me, and he knew that.

Anyway, right now I just wanted him with us when I told Linda. I had not considered that he was also very close to the girls, and that this would be very hard for him. Brother Alvin had lost his own son when the boy was fourteen, I think, and I know now that the current situation renewed his pain from that loss. I did not realize that at the time. I had been in Texarkana, and I was *literally* numb. I could not feel anything, and I failed to recognize that everyone else *could* feel pain.

When I got there I talked to him for about an hour. I told him enough about what I knew so that he would understand why I thought I needed him to help me. I should have realized that I was telling him way too much at one time. He would become very upset when he heard various things. It was like talking to Kim earlier that week, except that I offered *him* very little comfort.

I told him the police were close to arresting Jason. He asked me what kind of an engineer Jason was and some questions about the plant where he worked. Then he said, "If Jason did have something to do with it, we may never see that child again." He imagined Jason having access to places in the plant that contained all kinds of chemicals, saying that he could have disposed of her anywhere in there, and nobody would ever see her again. When a person is required to contemplate an unthinkable situation, he can't be held responsible for the images his mind contrives. This ordeal was evil and unnatural, and everyone involved had to struggle to stay sane and reasonable. As I said, I had asked too much of him, too soon. I talked for a long time and tried to come up with every logical reason why Jason could not have made such a plan work, even if he was involved. It was too risky for him. Jason had not been at GP very long and didn't really know the plant well. The conversation became something of a debate, but after a little while we both just let it go. This was Saturday afternoon, and he had already agreed to come over that night.

Like almost everything else that week, much of what I thought was necessary really was not.

When he got there that night, we all sat down, and I began to explain about the evidence the police had, saying that it was a real possibility they would arrest Jason. I was very intense and angry at that point. Linda was not impressed or bothered by what the police were going to do. She continued to maintain that Jason had not done anything and that Hollie would be found. Even if Hollie was dead, she believed that Jason was not involved. I was glad to be telling them anyway. By this point, Weslea was not surprised.

Brother Alvin explained the phases we would go through, and was very emotional as he talked. He said we would or could be angry at God and ourselves. He went over the many aspects of losing a loved one.

We talked for a long time. I remember saying over and over that if I could just know that Hollie was in no pain then I could handle my own pain. *If I could just know.*

As much as I believed it at the time, this was not altogether true. I have handled my pain poorly.

The next few days just kind of ran together. The only feeling I can remember is that of being in the wrong place all the time. I tried to work some on Monday and Tuesday. I didn't get anything done.

Hollie's friends who had worked so hard distributing the flyers thought it would be a good idea for us to have a mobile phone. They arranged for a local company in Texarkana to provide us with one. When we got back to Mississippi we could not find a local company that could tie into their bands or company there. I decided to get a pager. It took me all day Monday to find a pager. I went to four or five places and they all were the same. I just couldn't find one that was right. When I finally got one I called Lt. Satterfield and gave him the number. Linda had it, too. The lieutenant told me that if anything changed he would page me. *The pager took on the characteristics of a bomb.*

I was working at a subdivision called Summer Tree when Weslea paged me one afternoon. I went into the house to use the phone. Hollie and I had done work in the yard there last summer, and Hollie had cut the grass a few times.

I was hanging up the phone when the woman whose house it was walked through and asked if everything was O.K. I said something like, "Well, you know how daughters are." She said, "Tell Hollie hello for me when you see her." I just stood there as she walked out of the room. (A week or so after the funeral I went back to see her and to say I was sorry I didn't tell her that day. She felt very bad, but of course she hadn't known. I am glad I went back to see her.)

The one thing I remember about Monday and Tuesday is the rose that Linda found in the woods behind the house. I had thrown away some rose bushes that someone had discarded. Linda and Wes were walking back there and found a rose, the only one blooming on all those bushes.

It was pretty, yellow with red margins on each petal. Linda took a lot of comfort from the rose. She saw it as an omen that Hollie would be coming back, and she put it in a vase on the bar. When people would come over she would show it to them and say something like, "You see, we *will* find Hollie." If it had not made her feel this way I would have thrown it away. To me, it was as if the red on the petals had been poured on from the outside edge. I would look at it and think, "*Why does no one see the blood? Am I the only one who thinks this way? There is blood on this—on every petal. I don't believe in omens, but if this is one—it's bleeding. Is this Hollie's blood? Does it mean she's bleeding?*" I suppose no one else saw it that way. We left it out for a week, and I never got used to looking at the thing.

Maybe it did mean we would find her, and maybe that *was* blood.

I was getting ready to go back to Arkansas. I had been gone too long and felt like I needed to be there. I was to leave on Saturday. I had talked to the lieutenant only once since we got back. He called about mid-afternoon on Wednesday, and we talked for a while.

January 5, 1998

Christmas is over and I have decided to finish this story, even though in some ways it seems useless. This is the first time I have written anything since before Christmas. *Christmas was hard.* Having everyone around was good most of the time—change was good—but I think it left everyone feeling a little empty afterward.

Now, I will try to finish recording the conversation I had with Lt. Satterfield that Wednesday. *It has become so hard to do this.* I can't remember exactly what was said, but I can't stop thinking about writing down what I do remember.

PART FOUR

It's Over

April 19, 1997, Continued

Jason had been scheduled to take his second polygraph on the previous Wednesday. When I asked the lieutenant about it he told me that it was inconclusive. It was as if he had no feelings or reactions.

First, he told me they had been very busy working on the case. They had dragged a lake north of Texas, and that's where the mud on Jason's boots had come from. He and Hollie had been there a couple of weeks before. (He didn't tell me that the press had turned on Jason and was beginning to give him a very hard time.) He told me about some other leads. Then he got to the real reason he had called.

Satterfield: "We found a couple of bags of evidence thrown out beside the highway north of here—

close to Forman, Arkansas, about twenty miles from Texarkana."

Me: "What kind of evidence?"

Satterfield: "There were some of Hollie's things in two garbage bags."

Me: "What things?"

Satterfield: "I don't think I need to tell you. They were things that Hollie had with her the last time anyone saw her. I had rather not tell you."

Me: "When you find Hollie who will have to tell me?"

Satterfield: "I will."

Me: "If you can do that, you can do this. I will have to let you tell me when you do find her."

Satterfield: "I will go through this, and if you want me to stop, just tell me. If not, I will just list the articles for you."

Me: "I will stop you if I have to, or I will hang up or something. O.K.?"

Satterfield: "There were two bags—a kid found them on the side of the highway, and why he picked them up I'll never know. It's as though God just laid them out for us. Anyway, Hollie's shirt that she was last seen wearing, her pocketbook, her car keys, and her blue jeans were in there. Her blue jeans were cut up the seams from the bottom of the legs all the way up to her belt and the inside seams were cut up to the crotch. *There was no blood.* There was no blood on anything, not even her jeans. Her shoes—there were a couple of balls of duct tape balled up like, you know, you were throwing it away. There was what may be strands of Hollie's hair found in one of the balls. We're still going over this stuff for prints. Everything is at the lab now. Also, a couple of pair of panties and a bra. There was one end of a fish stringer, and it was cut about in half. There was mud on the jeans, shirt, and shoes."

Of all of it, I think the fish stringer bothered me the most.
The lieutenant was very precise when he told me about the different items and paused a little between each one, I think to give me an opportunity to stop him.

I was sitting on our back porch while I was talking to him; Linda was in the kitchen, and I was looking at her. Up until this time I had been able to talk to him without becoming emotional. *Today was no different.* The only problem I had was that as he talked I could feel my face changing. I could feel my mouth being drawn down, and I knew that, no matter how hard I tried, my expression was not going to change for a long, long time. It was like the feeling that shows in your face when you are looking at something so bad you would never want to see it if you had a choice, and you know that what you are seeing will not change no matter what you do or say—it is not fixable.

Previously when I had talked to Tom or the other policeman, I could see Hollie somewhere *alive* and maybe tied up—my mind would go through a scenario in which I could see her alive. *That did not happen this time.* He said there was no blood.

He told me that he had interviewed Jason for most of the

day after the polygraph. I asked if he had changed his mind. He said he had not. This was really hard for me to understand. He said that after a few hours of the interview when it seemed he was going nowhere, he took Hollie's keys out of his pocket, threw them on the table, and asked Jason if he knew what they were. Jason said, "They are Hollie's keys." He showed no emotion. Tom also showed him the blue jeans and got no response.

I said I didn't know what was wrong with Jason, but I was sure he had nothing to do with it. I had really given a lot of thought to the possibility of Jason doing this since I had been back home. Jason and Hollie as a couple had not left my mind since we left Texarkana on Friday. I knew that Jason had shut down to survive. My way of surviving was to talk and talk and talk. Everyone handles stress or a crisis in a different way. (The last time they had taken the boat out they stayed overnight on a lake near Texarkana. The nights were cold so they let two of the puppies sleep inside the tent with them. The other one slept at the door. I would go over Hollie's description of the outing in my mind, and I could see them over and over. To me this is not what murderers do on weekends. These were things a couple of newlyweds do. They were so silly with those puppies.) Then I asked him if it were not possible that some redneck had Hollie tied to a tree somewhere, maybe in the mountains north of there. He said that nothing pointed to that having happened, considering the physical evidence they had.

At the time I did not want to go into what he was talking about. I figured I had heard enough about evidence for a little while.

IT'S OVER

I told Linda the police had found some things of Hollie's beside the road. She asked for few details; hearing that much was all she could take at the time, I think.

Nothing happened Thursday and Friday. I made plans to go back to Texarkana Saturday morning and stay for a little while. Marvin, Linda's brother, wanted to go with me, or at least Linda wanted me to take him.

Saturday, April 26, 1997

The weather was terrible Friday night and Saturday morning as we left at about six o'clock to return to Texarkana. It was windy, raining, and turning cold. Marvin and I talked about almost everything on the way over. When we were halfway there I thought I had better tell him that the police had decided the first day that Jason had hurt Hollie. He didn't say much as I tried to explain what had happened. I didn't tell him a lot, but I said enough so that he could understand what was going on. I told him about some of the things the police had found in the bags. *I had to tell somebody, and I had not until now.*

We were about an hour and a half away when Linda called on the car phone and told me that Lt. Satterfield had called to tell us they had arrested somebody. He didn't give her a lot of details, only saying that someone had been arrested. He said he was sorry I was not there when he called.

Marvin and I were just north of the Louisiana state line when we got behind a log truck that was driving about forty-five miles per hour. For some reason I felt as though I should be there with Jason, as though I should have been there an hour ago. It was raining so hard I could hardly see the front of the log truck when I would pull out to pass and then have to dart back into my lane before an oncoming car could hit us. I began to tell Marvin about the logs, saying that they were probably going to the mill where Jason worked and telling him how many logs the mill processed. I described everything I knew about Jason's work while pointing at the logs from time to time. Then all of a sudden, I realized that the mill was past Texarkana. *We didn't have time to follow this truck another fifty miles.* I told Marvin he needed to fasten his seat belt; I was going to have to pass this truck. He asked if I could see the front of the truck. I said, "No—hold on to something." I continued talking. "Jason is totally committed to his work, and I think he will do well." As we were passing, spray hit our windshield in blasts as we went by each one of the wheels. I glanced over at Marvin and said, "Can you see the front of this truck yet?" He said, "What truck?"

Linda and Wanda got together and waited for Wes and Martin to get to Madison. Everybody felt the need to be in Texarkana as soon as they could get there. They started out later in the morning, and we kept in touch with them.

I called Jason immediately after I talked to Linda. He didn't know any more than she did. He was waiting for a call from the police.

Marvin and I arrived in Texarkana about twelve o'clock. I had driven much too fast in the rain to get there. When we got to Jason's house, he told us a little more. He was still waiting to be called back.

The phone rang shortly after we arrived, and I answered it. It was the lieutenant calling for Jason.

He told me he was sorry that he had missed me earlier that morning. I said that my timing wasn't so good but that I was ready to hear now.

Satterfield: "Jason didn't have anything to do with it, and I apologized to him this morning. We have arrested a man who has admitted that he kidnapped Hollie."

Me: "Do you believe him? He is not some nut who wants his picture in the paper, is he?"

Satterfield: "Based on his confession and the physical evidence we have, we have locked him up and charged him with *kidnapping* and *murder.*"

Me: "I see."

Satterfield: "We arrested him last night, and we were with him all night. I called your wife before I went to bed this morning. I have just gotten up, and I am on my way back down to the station now."

Me: "Where is Hollie?"

Satterfield: "We don't know yet. He says he can't remember. He said he was high when he took her and doesn't remember what he did with her. He's an old, burned-out dopehead, and he was looking for money to get another fix. He thought Hollie's car was a fifty-thousand-dollar car, and the way Hollie was dressed he knew she had money—*the coat— the leather coat.*"

Me: "What about Hollie."

Satterfield: "I'm going to have to stay with him until he tells me where she is. Right now he thinks I am his friend. I give him cigarettes. I am going to have to kiss his butt until he tells me where she is; I'm not sure I can do that."

Me: "You have to do that. You told me you would find her. You told me that the first day. You have to do whatever it takes. I will do anything I can to help you. I will bring you coffee, guns, or anything, but you have to stay with him until he tells you. That's why we are here—to get Hollie."

Satterfield: "I'm going back now, and I'll be with him the rest of the day. I'll find her."

The phone I was using was an old one with a cord, and it was on the floor by the sofa. When I answered it, I was leaning over a little to talk, because the phone was still on the floor, but when I finished the conversation and hung it up I was on my knees with the phone receiver almost in my lap. The longer I talked the closer to the floor I got. I just kept bending over.

When I hung up I looked up at Marvin and Jason. Jason didn't say anything. Marvin looked at me and said, "We still have to tell Linda."

I couldn't say anything. I just thought, *"That was the worst part of anything that could have ever happened to anybody, any-where. The man has just told me that my daughter has been kid-napped and murdered by some son-of-a-bitch who doesn't even know what he did with her body—he killed her because he wanted a fix and she was dressed well."* Marvin meant no harm; he just could not comprehend what was going on here.

The lieutenant told us that the media would be all over the place later that day when they released the informa-tion about their arrest. Jason and Diane went over to the GP house so the press could not find him.

Marvin and I waited for the others—Linda, Wanda, Weslea, and Martin. They did not get there until about six o'clock, having run into a lot of rain on the way. So Marvin and I sat there all afternoon. It rained and rained.

We had the TV on with no sound, just the picture, at six o'clock when the news came on. I was standing by the big windows looking at it. A picture of the man who murdered Hollie came on. We turned the sound up, and they showed his picture again. They also showed timberland where apparently they thought Hollie was, but the images of him and the place where she might be were so overwhelming that I just shut down. I didn't know what they said.

Soon after the news was over Linda and Weslea arrived. Wes and Martin parked in front of the house, on the street, and Linda parked behind them. As Wes was getting out and walking up to the house, a couple was going with their two children down the sidewalk, close to where the cars were parked. They apparently had seen the news. As Wes walked across in front of them, the man said, "I'm sorry for what happened." He started to say something else, but Weslea held her hand up to her face a little, looked down, and told him, "I'm sorry. We don't know anything yet; my Dad has to tell us. I'm sorry." *I watched them pass by. The man and I just looked at each other.*

They all came in, and I stood in front of the fireplace. They all huddled around me, as if we were going to say a prayer.

I repeated what I had been told. The only part I had trouble with was when I said, "They charged him with *murder*—and they are pretty sure that's what happened."

After that we all got ready to go to the GP house. We were leaving when a friend of Hollie's and her husband came in the back to pick up the puppies. I went to let them in, and they had not heard anything, so I stood in the kitchen and told them. *I looked at them; they were so young.* I had such a hard time telling them. I just couldn't seem to finish what I was saying, and they couldn't seem to say anything at all. They really never said much of anything.

January 18, 1998

Saturday, April 26, 1997, Continued

It must have been about seven o'clock when we all got to the GP house. *Being there was really bad; it was like going back to the last week.* Everybody picked out a bedroom, and no one chose the same room they had had the week before. I suppose that everyone felt as I did about being there. No one had really expected to have to come back to this place.

Jason's boss, Rose, had arranged for our food to be brought in. Various people had made dishes. About nine or ten o'clock that night the lieutenant called, saying that he wanted to come by and tell us about the search.

He looked very tired. He had on a police jacket, boots, and a cap. He didn't drink coffee; that seemed strange to me. We all sat down at a big conference table, which was in a sunroom at the back of the house. He sat at the head of the table.

Everyone seemed to have questions for him about where they were looking and about the murderer. He tried to explain where the search was, but I couldn't concentrate on geographics long enough to understand where they were searching in relation to where we were.

He told us that the murderer thought that he, the lieutenant, was his friend and that legally he could keep the murderer until he found Hollie. There were several charges against this man. He said there were so many people at the search area that the murderer was scared, and that he was going to organize the people a little better tomorrow so there would be fewer people around at the scene.

I told the lieutenant I didn't see how he could stay in the car with this man as he had to do. He said we had to remember that the murderer had two small children and had only been married for about one year to his second wife.

I suppose he couldn't think of anything else to tell me about the man. I realized that I was about to come unscrewed, again, and I thought that he would not want that to happen—not with the whole family sitting there. He looked at me as he spoke even when he answered someone else's question.

You see, as he talked I heard very little of what he said. He was exhausted, mad, and doing a good job of explaining as much as he could in order to satisfy everyone—to some extent. When I looked at him, I knew that no matter what he said he hated to go back and be with the murderer again tomorrow. You could see the disgust and anger on his face. The only thing I could think of was that he had to go from being in the car with someone who had confessed

murdering a *daughter* to her parents and family and try
and explain to them what he had to do. I do not to this day
understand the mind-set someone would have to have to
make that transition. The look on his face almost put me in
the car with the two of them; I could practically hear the
murderer talking about killing Hollie. I could hardly get
myself through this meeting. It had become *too* personal
over the last two weeks, and he knew it, because he had
talked to a lot of her friends and to the people she and
Jason had gone out with. He knew that Hollie loved to
wear hats. In all the pictures he had of Hollie, she was
smiling, and she looked like his daughter. I could not have
known her that well and done what he had to do. I can't
imagine what it must have been like listening to a murderer talking and suddenly realizing that he had done what
he was confessing to.

*It is the most helpless feeling known to a human—it's after the
fact.*

I suppose I remember more about how he looked than
what he said, which seemed immaterial. I understood that
they knew enough to find her, or I thought I did.

He told us that he would keep in touch with us Sunday
and let us know what they were doing and where. I told
him that it was not necessary. We knew where he was,
and it would only be inconvenient for him to call us. "Just
look for Hollie and do what you have to do to deal with
it," I said.

Everybody thanked him for what he was doing. He
shook Jason's hand, and then he shook mine. When he
took my hand he pulled me in to him and hugged me.
He is a big man and it wasn't hard for him to do.

My knees nearly buckled, and I almost lost it. He had to do that for himself. *It had become almost too hard for either of us to deal with the process.*

January 21,1998

Sunday, April 27, 1997

Morning

T he lieutenant called about eight o'clock Sunday morning to get permission to take the murderer back to Hollie's. He and Tom were going to walk the man through the whole thing step by step.

We did not hear from him again until late Sunday night.

It rained all day Sunday. People brought in food, and some just came by to see us. It was very hard to talk to them. What were we supposed to talk about? Hollie, I guess. One lady whom Hollie had talked to at the hospital about her major or some social work jobs had gotten to know her well, and she just wanted to meet us. *God, it was so hard to sit there and talk to her.* Hollie had told me who she was and what she did. I wanted to say, "Wait just a minute and I'll go get Hollie. She would like to talk to you about her school work and her career."

Linda would leave the room when these people came in. I think she was having a hard time figuring out why they kept coming by. It didn't seem to be a thing to do.

———

There was one duck on the lake that was swimming by himself away from all the other ducks. I watched him on and off all day and never could figure out why he would not go over with the other ducks.
Ducks like the rain.

———

We sat all day Sunday, talking to each other very little. We spoke to the people who came in. The rest of the time we watched it rain and rain and rain. *God, did it rain.* How could they possibly find anything in this weather? Between Friday night and Monday morning, it rained six inches.

Linda spent a lot of the day in her room. She simply could not deal with all the people.

Weslea left Sunday afternoon; Martin had a test on Monday. I was glad she left. We had no idea how long we would be there. Sitting there and doing nothing was almost more than she could bear, and there was absolutely nothing we could do now. I think that Wes just wanted to get away from us so she could cry if she wanted. She never cried around us. Now, I wish I had sat down with her and told her that it was O.K. if she cried—she could cry all day.

I never did that. I'm sure she thought we would fall apart if she did.

Marvin and Wanda were a lot of help, just because they were there. Jason did not talk much unless someone asked him a specific question. I can only imagine how hard this was for him. Wanda was helpful in talking to some of the people who came by. Sometimes I would just walk away from them, especially as it got later in the day.

We watched the news that night, and they showed Hollie's picture again and the same timberland scene.

Night

The lieutenant called about ten o'clock. They had not found anything, but he was encouraged because the search was better organized and the murderer had given them more information during their walk- through that morning. He felt like they were making progress. They had pinned the area down to one section, but the weather was making it slow going.

We went to bed about twelve or one o'clock that night. I really just lay there and listened to the rain and imagined the people working in it tomorrow. I was worried they would stop looking, or that Hollie would wash away before it stopped.

Linda and I talked very little; we just lay there and held onto each other. I think at some point that night we both went to sleep.

Monday, April 28, 1997

When we got up Monday it had stopped raining. We ate breakfast and started getting ready to leave. The house was needed for some people coming in that night, so GP had arranged for us to stay at the Holiday Inn Express in Texarkana.

After breakfast Jason, Diane, Linda, and I sat down together and talked about where we would bury Hollie. It was Jason's decision, and we all felt the time had come to discuss it. Linda and I had talked about it, and I told her that she would have to get Jason to let Hollie be taken back to Madison. I knew he would do what Linda wanted. *He owed her that.* He spoke of having her buried in south Mississippi with his father, or in Texarkana, close by him. I mentioned that he might be transferred, and Diane told him that he could move Hollie and take her with him. This was the hardest part of the conversation, to say the least. Jason finally decided to let us take her to Madison as Linda wanted. It was strange to be having this conversation.

We moved to the motel. Our rooms were next to a small conference room with a sofa, table, chairs, and refrigerator. Even though the individual rooms were close by and gave us some privacy, everyone either stayed in the conference room or went in and out. It was as though you knew that whatever was going to happen would happen here. I can't remember going into our room all day. We didn't have enough keys to the conference room, so we propped the door open. No one wanted to bother letting people in repeatedly. That's where we spent most of Monday morning.

It was a nice motel. The conference room had a small balcony; when you stood on it you could see a large building that joined the motel on the back. It had tinted windows and was about the size of a gymnasium.

I was standing out there when someone walked outside. They pointed and asked what that building might be. I told them that it was an indoor pool with weight rooms and such. I had heard that it was very nice. I remembered a conversation I had had with Hollie last fall.

"Hello."

"Hey, what are you doing?"

"I'm eating lunch. What are you doing?"

"Where are you? You still in Arkansas?"

"I'm at the Holiday Inn Express in Texarkana. Jason is in a new employees' orientation. I've been swimming all morning. They have a real nice indoor heated pool. It's behind the motel in a big building, with tinted windows all around it—really big—must be corporate. I wanted to ask you what you thought about some of these houses we've looked at."

"You've only been there for two days. You're buying a house already? Do you think you may be rushing it a bit?"

"Well, Jason wants to buy us a house. We need a house, you know. Anyway, let me tell you what I did this morning. Jason was running a little late when he left, and he forgot his briefcase. I saw it about five minutes later, so I put my hair under my cap and thought I would catch him and give it to him before he left the motel. When I ran past the lobby I saw him sitting with some little businessmen—he was so cute sitting there being corporate—so I ran over and gave him his briefcase. I was so proud of myself for taking care of him that way. Jason looked at me, then he looked at my feet. I had my cap on backwards, cut-off blue jeans, a T-shirt and no shoes. I looked around at all those businessmen and got tickled. "

"I think you're going to have to work on the corporate wife image, don't you?"

"Yes, maybe in my spare time. Jason's going to help. We're going to get dressed up tonight and go to a GP party for new people. Jason and I clean up real good. GP gave Jason a corporate credit card and we eat steak every meal. Now, let me tell you about this house—see what you think. O.K.?"

Wanda interrupted my thoughts to tell me that the pastor from Jason's church was here and that he wanted to say a prayer with us. I said O.K. *We prayed.*

I thought that I would have to go and see the federal prosecutor, so that afternoon I went and bought a shirt. *I am now using it as a target when I shoot my bow.* I had only brought one with me. I never did plan to stay any length of time when I came here. *It always seemed wrong to plan to stay.*

Late that afternoon a group from Jason's church came by and brought food. There always seemed to be someone bringing food. There must have been eight or ten people in the group. I remember thinking how small the room had gotten since earlier in the day.

Before they left, one of the men wanted to say a prayer for us. He began to pray, and the only thing I remember him saying was, *"God, please forgive me. I know I am inadequate."* I thought, "How can he feel that way?" Maybe there was always something inadequate about my prayers. I thought, "Dear God, all I have said when I prayed was, *God, please help Hollie,* and *God, please help me through this day."* I prayed for nothing else and could not think of anything else to say to Him. I made no promises or apologies. I would scream to Him and say, "*Help me—please. We have to find Hollie. Don't let her hurt anymore.*" *What if that was inadequate? What if I had said that wrong? You can only scream so loud in your mind and say a limited number of words. I thought that maybe He didn't hear me.*

I had asked for Hollie not to be cold, and she wasn't cold. I had asked that she not be in pain, and she wasn't. I had asked that she not be afraid and she wasn't—she was with Him, and I know that. All of my prayers were for me and the family, but they were loud and short. Maybe I shouldn't have screamed— maybe I should have sat down somewhere and just talked to God. Maybe you can't wait until you feel you have to scream before you talk to Him. The strange thing is I got everything I asked for, but it was after the fact. Maybe I should have asked sooner. Is this what the man meant when he said he was inadequate? Probably not.

Rose came by early that evening after the group had left. She brought food and a coffee maker. Rose seemed to know what we needed at any given time. Jason had always said she was a *good* boss.

This was a really big coffee maker with lots of parts. A couple of Jason's friends were there. They all started to put this thing together. It must have had four pages of instructions and they wanted to read every word. We all began to wonder how long it was going to take four engineers to put a coffee pot together. Marvin had bought a small one earlier. He is not an engineer, but while they were working on theirs Marvin put his together and made us a cup of coffee. We drank coffee as they toiled away with the instructions; it became quite a joke.

Rose's husband came with her. He is from the mountain country of eastern Tennessee, and she is from Pennsylvania. He began to tell us about some of their cultural differences and what their life was like early in their marriage. His stories were quite comical, and it was enjoyable listening to him talk in his eastern Tennessee accent.

He began to tell me with much enthusiasm about his hunting trips into the mountains. As I listened to him I could see the mountains and feel the cold wind. It was as though he were saying, *"You look like you need to walk through the mountains with me for a little while. You will feel better, and you can come back anytime you like."* I would ask enough questions to keep him talking, because every so often I would feel the wind and see the deer.

Then I would come back to that room, and I would want to say, *"I have to be alone, now—I need to cry, and scream at God, and cuss everybody. God, if I don't scream, or cry, or something, I really do think I am going to die in this room. I have to do this alone—away from anyone. This is between me and God and Hollie."* But I never said anything, and he never stopped talking. I would concentrate on his words again and let him take me back to those cold, windy mountains. It was another place and another time, and it was good there. Maybe he just wanted to take me to his *safe* place. *He and Rose have one child—a daughter.*

April 28, 1998

for some reason I have felt for a long time now that it was necessary for me to finish writing this. It was something like writing a really long outline. I will probably go back and fill in some blanks, but I feel much better that I did at least finish it.

I think it is important for me to describe how everybody reacted. Judi told me once that I would need to write Hollie a letter. I think maybe this is what my little story turned out to be. I felt very bad about some of the things I did and said, regarding, for example, Jason. I felt worse about not ever really getting out and physically looking for Hollie. It is very hard to explain because I had thought that would be my *only* reaction. I could hardly say the name "Hollie." I could not look at the people whose reaction to me was either fear or pity when I would ask if they had seen her. It was as if I could not tell them enough about Hollie. *How could you not know Hollie?* I wasn't so out of it that I could not have done that. Anyway, maybe I was trying to apologize to Hollie for something I did *not* do. The worst thing was not the process or the time we spent there, but the realization that Hollie was not coming back no matter what I did or said. I was so confused about where she was and what she could see. I knew she was gone, but I could not figure out the technicality of Heaven, or if it hurt.

I think it may have been of some consolation to me to think I still had some effect on what she may have thought or how she felt. This was so much in my own mind that I am still afraid someone will put me away someday. Surely, there are more direct ways to get to where you are going. *The thoughts I had in order to keep some sort of connection with her scare me*—mainly because I can't believe I thought that way to begin with.

Being alone is not good for anyone ever, but being alone in a crisis like that and not letting anyone in was my biggest mistake.

After the Funeral...

Kim called me one night two weeks after the funeral. It was about one o'clock, and I had been asleep for awhile. When I answered the phone she was crying and kind of screamed into the phone, saying, "Keith, I am so sorry." I thought she was Weslea's mother-in-law and that something had happened to Weslea. When I asked who she was, she regained her composure, and we started the conversation over. We talked until four-thirty in the morning, about everything. I think this was one of Kim's worst times. She had been back home long enough to feel really isolated, and she was getting very little help from the people around her.

She asked me how I stood it. "How do you think about it?" she asked. "How do you think about Hollie?" She understood what I told her.

I said that it was like taking your family to a drive-in movie in days past. You park somewhere close to the screen, and then you go to the concession stand to get everybody something to eat. You are in there for awhile because you have to get something for everyone. Then you start back with all those little cardboard containers. The movie has started, and you turn to watch it. It's the "Hollie movie." You just stand there, *unable to look away*. The movie consists of clips of Hollie's life as you knew it, each one lasting for maybe five to ten seconds. You see her when she was in the band and when she was two, when she was getting married, sleeping late, and laughing with her mouth full. The clips seem to come at random—they are just little things that you happen to remember. Then there's a picture of the murderer—*then Hollie running and being shot*. (For a long time I always saw her being shot at some point after I had seen his face, which was the picture they showed on TV the day Marvin and I went back to Texarkana. After the murderer I always saw the blood and I thought that I would never go through the sequence without seeing it, but at some point I eliminated him and the blood from my memories of Hollie.) But it never ends with that; there is always a final clip in which she is smiling. The movie comes full circle and starts over.

Standing there you realize that all the stuff you are carrying is beginning to melt and ruin, but you can't look down, and you can't seem to look for your car— you just stand there. It's as if you can't turn away because if you do you will miss one of the clips, and it may never be shown again and you will forget it. You know that time will make you forget. It doesn't matter—you can't move. You know you have to find your car before everything is ruined. They're all waiting for you there.

When I described this to Kim I didn't use quite as much detail, and I didn't mention the murderer. She understood and never asked me again. I told her that when I was better and could turn away, I would let her know that I had found my car.

I had no hope at the time that I would ever find my car. I did, but it was very different and a little beat up. It amazes me that there is a void not only for Hollie, but everywhere in my life.

Attitude

I talked to Tom McCollum last summer, and he told me most of the details about what had happened to Hollie. He told me that she had handled herself well, that much of what she had done was due to the fact that she was strong, and that her training and what she had learned in school had influenced her reactions.

You see, I had no idea what her school work was like, not a clue. I really couldn't get a grip on how it all related.

I realize now that it is an attitude not a course of study. I found her *attitude.*

The fact that it did *not* save her is something that I will have to deal with, like the fact that she got some of it from me, or maybe she just listened to a part of me that I didn't realize I was making so loud.

Anyway, it is not a question at this time.

PART FIVE

Her Name is Hollie

August 12, 1975

D r. Cook, who always looked so serious walked down the hall that connected the delivery to the waiting room. I wondered why they made these halls so long. I had been staring at those doors for what seemed like a very long time.

He finally reached me, smiled, and told me that I had another beautiful daughter. There were no life or death decisions to be made—none of the complications that I had imagined while I waited. Now if I could see her I would be O.K. Dr. Cook told me that they would bring her into the nursery in a few minutes, and I could see her then.

When I stood there looking through the glass at three newborns, I wondered if I should just pick one of them out, point at it, and tell the nurses that I would take that one.

They let me into the nursery, and making my selection was no problem.

She was the first baby I saw. They had put her into an incubator and had her head elevated slightly. I wondered if she had a problem breathing, but she looked so comfortable that I soon stopped worrying.

I stood there, watching her drift into sleep and then waken for a little while. She was such a big baby. There was not one hair on her head. She looked so clean.

She was waking and moving around somewhat. The nurses asked if I would like to hold her. I sat down in a rocking chair, and they gave her to me. I touched her for the first time. As I began to rock, she just lay there and looked at me, making those little gurgling sounds that only babies can make. She was so content.

I rocked and rocked. We became quite comfortable, and after a little while, we talked with each other for the first time.

Her name was Hollie

Print Media Coverage

Because it was so difficult to write the details of what happened, I have included newspaper articles from the *Texarkana Gazette* which will give readers a clear account of the sequence of events.

POLICE THINK MISSING WOMAN WAS ABDUCTED

By Lori Dunn
Of the Gazette Staff

Texarkana, Ark, police believe a woman reported missing Friday may have been abducted. Hollie Calhoun Miller, 21, was reported missing Friday night by her husband, Jason Miller. "We are working this as an abduction or kidnapping. We have not ruled anything out," said Sgt. Glen Greenwell, Arkansas-side police spokesman. Greenwell said officers are trying to establish a time line and need information from people who might have seen Hollie Miller or had contact with her since Friday morning. Greenwell said Office Bobby Jordan talked to Jason Miller at his home in the 2000 block of Laurel Street about 9 p.m. Friday when he first reported his wife missing. Jason Miller told Jordan he left for work about 7 a.m. Friday and his wife still was at home. He said his wife had an 8 a.m. job interview at a day care center. Police confirmed that Hollie Miller went to the interview. Jason Miller told police that his wife called him at work about

9:30 a.m. but he was unable to take the call. He tried to call her at home several times during the day but always got a busy signal. "He told the officers he was not concerned about that because he thought the dog had knocked the phone off the hook," Greenwell said.

Hollie Miller was not at home when her husband returned from work. Her purse was missing but her car was in the driveway.

Greenwell said Jason Miller realized something might be wrong when he discovered a package of CPC cigarettes on the kitchen counter, because he and his wife do not smoke.

A long, blonde wig was discovered in the bedroom.

Jason Miller told police there were no signs of forced entry and the house did not look as though a struggle had taken place.

But officers have discovered information that leads them to believe Hollie Miller was abducted.

"We have discovered things that have us very concerned and make us think foul play was involved. This is more than a woman who just left home," Greenwell said.

SEARCH FOR MISSING ARKANSAS WOMAN CONTINUES

By Russell Minor
Of the Gazette Staff

Investigators continue using cadaver dogs to scour the banks of the Red River as the search for a Texarkana, Ark., woman who mysteriously disappeared 11 days ago continues with no significant leads or suspects. Hollie Miller, 21, disappeared from her 2001 Laurel St. home April 11, likely in the late morning or early afternoon, police said. Her husband, reportedly an engineer at Georgia-Pacific, returned home from work to find Hollie Miller gone but her car still at the home. A package of GPC cigarettes rested on the kitchen counter. Neither the husband nor wife smoked. A blond wig was discovered in the bedroom. Reported missing from the residence was a blue G-P duffel bag, Hollie Miller's undergarments from a dresser drawer, Jason Miller's leather wallet, which contained only a set of keys to his vehicle, and a long black trench coat from a hall closet. Other articles of clothing and personal items were not missing. Investigators interviewed the victim's husband, Jason Miller, the night he reported his wife missing on April 11. Police learned the victim completed a job interview at a local day care center, went home and changed clothes. The tan dress Hollie Miller wore to the interview was found in the bedroom underneath a wadded pair of pantyhose. A few days later, police conducted a search of the home. The search uncovered new evidence, but police remain mum on what the evidence was or what it means. "Right now, we can't talk about any of that," said Sgt. Glenn Greenwell. As the search for Hollie Miller continues, police still are trying to learn what happened on the day the victim disappeared. Greenwell said the case is being worked by investigators in crimes against persons and is being treated as a kidnapping and possible homicide. "But, really, we don't know what happened," he said. The Millers' residence showed no signs of forced entry or of a struggle on April 11.

MISSING WOMAN'S BILLFOLD PROVIDES LEAD IN MILLER CASE

By Russell Minor
Of the Gazette Staff

The first significant lead in the search for a Texarkana, Ark., woman who mysteriously vanished April 11 turned up Wednesday when a man stumbled upon the missing woman's billfold near a cemetery in Fulton, Ark. Texarkana, Ark., police believe the discovery is "a turning point" in their quest to learn what happened to 21-year-old Hollie Miller. "This is a difficult case and we have a number of officers working continuously to get it solved," said Sgt. Glenn Greenwell, police spokesman. While the discovery does not point to a suspect, it does offer the first lead in a case that has delivered few clues. Police say a probe of the couple's home has not uncovered any fingerprints or other forensic evidence that points to a suspect. A blond wig and a package of GPC cigarettes found in the house may have belonged to the abductor,"...and, then again, they may have been used to throw police off the trail," Greenwell said. The lack of clues and suspects makes Wednesday's discovery even more important, he said. A man accidentally found Miller's billfold on a roadside Wednesday morning and took it to a clerk at a nearby store. The clerk recognized Miller's name and picture in the billfold and called police. The man reportedly told the clerk there were more items in the cemetery. In searching the area, investigators discovered articles of clothing believed to belong to Miller. Greenwell said police are no closer to solving the case or finding Miller, but added the new evidence may "shed a little light" on the investigation. The abduction occurred shortly after Miller arrived home from a job interview on April 11. Police found no signs of forced entry or signs of a struggle in the home. Miller's car remained parked at the house when her husband Jason Miller arrived home from work. Miller told police the blond wig found did not belong to his wife. He also told police the cigarettes found did not belong to him or his wife and that the couple do not smoke. "Several officers are taking this case personally," said Sgt. Shawn Vaughn. "They are working nonstop to solve this."

WOOLDRIDGE CHARGED WITH ABDUCTION AND HOMICIDE

By Lori Dunn
Of the Gazette Staff

Two weeks after a Texarkana, Ark., woman disappeared from her home, police have charged a man with her abduction and homicide. Steven Wayne Wooldridge, 41, of Wake Village, Texas, was arrested Friday night after he told police he was responsible for the disappearance of Hollie Miller, Texarkana, Ark., Police Chief Bob Harrison said in a press conference Saturday afternoon. Wooldridge first became a suspect when a man found Miller's wallet and several items of clothing Wednesday in a wooded area near Fulton, Ark. Harrison said a receipt in the bag of clothing showed evidence of a purchase that led police to Wooldridge. "It was a hunch that we looked into and we discovered the suspect had a prior record," Harrison said. Wooldridge is on parole in Texas for the abduction and attempted rape of a Houston woman in 1992. His parole officer is out of town and police have little infor-

mation about that crime or Wooldridge's incarceration. Police brought Wooldridge to Texarkana from a bakery in Hope where he is employed and he reportedly confessed after an interrogation. "He was nervous but he volunteered all of the information. He said there were things the police needed to know," Harrison said. Wooldridge told police he did not rape Miller. Police have the gun Wooldridge allegedly used, but Harrison declined to say what type of weapon it is or where Miller was shot. "There are a lot of things we want to release now but cannot," Harrison said. He said more details would be available later in the week. Harrison said Miller' father is already in Texarkana and knows about the arrest. Her mother and sister were on their way Saturday afternoon. Miller, 21, was reported missing April 11 by her husband Jason Miller, who cooperated fully with the police during the investigation. Harrison said Wooldridge is a drug addict who was looking for money to buy drugs on the afternoon of April 11. He reportedly was driving around the neighborhood in his 1978 Dodge van when he noticed

Article continued on following page

Miller in the yard of her home in the 2000 block of Laurel Street. "He circled the house a few times, parked away from the house, then approached Hollie and asked her if he could use her phone. She said yes," Harrison said. Once inside the house Wooldridge allegedly tied Miller's hands and took several items, including a Georgia Pacific tote bag filled with her underwear and a coat. He reportedly left his cigarettes and a blond wig inside the house. Police believe he may have brought the wig in case he needed a disguise to get into the house. Wooldridge told police he forced Miller outside and into her car and then drove the car to a storage room he had rented. He told police Miller rode in the front seat but the seat was reclining back. Wooldridge told police he left Miller in the storage room and drove her car back to her home before returning to the storage area in his van. Harrison said Wooldridge than drove out state Highway 8, where he shot Miller once and left her on the side of the road. Police have not yet recovered Miller's body. Wooldridge told police he was not familiar with the area and was not sure of the exact location. "It could be anywhere between Maud and Douglassville. We have people out searching the area and hopefully we will find something soon," Harrison said. Harrison said the storage room had been rented in Wooldridge's name for several months, and several items form a recent burglary were inside. "This has been a difficult case. There has been a new twist every day and we are sad for Hollie's family," Harrison said. Wooldridge is being held in the Bi-State Justice Center jail and bond has not been set. Harrison said he hoped people would be cautious when dealing with strangers. "We need to encourage people to be more cautious even though I like to believe we live in a safe community." Harrison said.

WOOLDRIDGE DEFENSE PLANS TO USE MENTAL EVALUATION

By Lisa Bose McDermott
Of the Gazette Staff

Although it still lacks the mental evaluation report, Steven Wooldridge's defense team intends to use the mental illness defense in the June 8 federal kidnapping and murder trial. Wooldridge, 42, is accused of kidnapping Hollie Calhoun Miller, 21, of Texarkana, Ark., on April 11, 1997. Miller was found dead in Cass County, Texas, on April 27, 1997. Miller's body was discovered two days after local police arrested Wooldridge, a Wake Village, Texas, resident. Federal prosecutors believe Wooldridge also killed Miller. They are seeking the death penalty against Wooldridge. Wooldridge's state of mind will be an issue in the case. In October, Wooldridge's lawyers, Barry Bryant and Craig Henry, filed a notice stating they intended to introduce testimony relating to mental disease that may bear upon Wooldridge's guilt or innocence. Bryant said the defense team's mental evaluation is complete although he does not have the results. The prosecution's psychologist completed its exam last week. The case's prosecution and defense met last week with U.S. District Judge Harry F. Barnes in El Dorado. Barnes set a June 8 trial date. David Blackorby, the lead prosecutor, could not be reached for comment. Brent Haltom, who was appointed special assistant U.S. attorney for the case, said he had not officially heard the case had been set. Bryant thinks it will take about one and one-half days to pick a jury in the case. Because it is in Texarkana, Ark., federal court, jurors will come from several counties including Miller and Lafayette counties. "I think it will take five to six days of court time," Bryant said.

FEDERAL PROSECUTORS AWAIT APPROVAL TO SEEK DEATH PENALTY AGAINST WOOLDRIDGE

By Lisa Bose McDermott
Of the Gazette Staff

If everything goes as planned, federal prosecutors will have their third death penalty case in Arkansas this year. Federal prosecutors from the Western District of Arkansas are awaiting approval from U.S. Attorney General Janet Reno to seek the death penalty against Steven Wayne Wooldridge. Wooldridge is believed to have kidnapped and murdered Hollie Miller, a 21-year-old Texarkana, Ark., resident. A criminal complaint of kidnapping was filed against Wooldridge by U.S. Attorney P.K. Holmes, and an indictment is expected as well. Miller is believed to have been abducted April 11 from her Laurel Street home. Her body was found April 28 in Cass County, Texas. Because the alleged abduction and murder took place in two different states, the case is being prosecuted by the U.S. Attorney's Office in Fort Smith. Cass County District Attorney Randal Lee previously cited the enormous expense that goes along with trying a murder case as a reason that it should be handled by federal prosecutors. The appellate process also has been mentioned by law enforcement officials as a reason to go the federal route. If Wooldridge is indicted and convicted in federal court, there are fewer chances for him to appeal than is he were tried in state court. Federal convicts lose the ability to appeal in state courts and in essence the appellate process is halved. Bill Cromwell, assistant U.S. attorney, said this is the third homicide case that will be tried in the Western District of Arkansas. In May and June, two men were tried and convicted in Hot Springs for the robbery and death of an 82-year-old man. One man received life in prison while the second man received the death penalty. Cromwell said it is unusual that there have been three federal cases involving homicides so close together.

WOOLDRIDGE MAKES FIRST APPEARANCE IN FEDERAL COURT AFTER FILED COMPLAINT

By Lisa Bose McDermott
Of the Gazette Staff

Friday was Steven Wayne Wooldridge's first appearance in federal court following a federal criminal complaint filed against him for his alleged abduction of Hollie Miller. U.S. Attorney P.K. Holmes of the Western District of Arkansas filed a criminal complaint against Wooldridge, 42, of Wake Village, on July 29. Wooldridge allegedly abducted Miller, 21, of Texarkana, Ark., from her Laurel Street home on April 11. Wooldridge also is the chief suspect in Miller's murder. Miller was found dead April 28 in Cass County, Texas. The federal complaint lists only a kidnapping charge against Wooldridge. Assistant U.S. Attorney Bill Cromwell said the complaint was filed simply to get Wooldridge into the federal system until Wooldridge's case could be presented to a grand jury for consideration. On Friday, U.S. Magistrate Bobby E. Shepherd appointed Barry Bryant, a Texarkana lawyer, to represent Wooldridge until other arrangements are made. Under the circumstances, Shepherd said Wooldridge will be eligible to have two lawyers represent him. He was declared indigent so the government will pick up the tab for his legal fees. Wooldridge told Shepherd he understood the charge against him. But Bryant asked for a hearing before Shepherd to decide probable cause to charge Wooldridge. This is something normally decided by a grand jury. Wooldridge also has kidnapping charges pending against him in Miller County, where he has been held without bond since his April 25 arrest. No murder charges have been filed against him in state or federal court. Cromwell said there was no need to add murder charges in the criminal complaint. That likely would be included in the indictment that prosecutors are anticipating will be handed down against Wooldridge. The only mention of the slaying was the statement in the complaint that Miller's body was found on April 28. However, prosecutors can hold Wooldridge responsible for

Article continued on following page

Miller's death if a grand jury
indicts him on a charge of kidnapping resulting in death. That
would allow federal prosecutors
to seek the death penalty against
Wooldridge. Cromwell said they
are waiting for approval from
U.S. Attorney General Janet Reno
to seek the death penalty against
Wooldridge.

HOLLIE MILLER TAKEN FROM HOME, SLAIN

By Lori Dunn
Of the Gazette Staff

When Steven Wayne Wooldridge allegedly abducted Hollie Miller from her home on Laurel Street and allegedly murdered her in Cass County, he also stole a little bit of Texarkana's innocence. Many believed it was the type of crime that could have never happened here. Miller, 21, was reported missing by her husband, Jason on April 11. She had gone to a job interview that morning and when her husband tried to call her later in the day he could not reach her. When Jason Miller arrived home that afternoon he discovered his wife was missing but that her car was still in the driveway. There was no sign of forced entry but there was a pack of GPC cigarettes on the kitchen counter and a long blonde wig in the bedroom. Officers from the Texarkana, Ark., Police Department's Crimes Against Persons unit began investigating Miller's disappearance and within two weeks had a suspect. Miller's wallet and a bag of clothing were found in a wooded area

in Fulton, Ark. A receipt discovered in the bad had Wooldridge's name on it. When police ran a check on the name they discovered Wooldridge was on parole in Texas for the abduction and attempted rape of a Houston woman in 1992. Police located Wooldridge working at a bakery in Hope, Ark., and after an interrogation he confessed that he had kidnapped and murdered Miller. He told police he has been looking for money to buy drugs when he spotted Miller in her yard. He asked her if he could use the phone and she let him into her home. Once inside the house, Wooldridge said he tied Miller's hands and took several items, including a Georgia-Pacific tote bag filled with her underwear and a coat. He left the cigarettes and wig inside the house. Police believe he brought the wig in case he needed a disguise to get into the house. Wooldridge told police he locked Miller in a storage building he had rented and then drover her car back to Laurel Street to get his van. He then said he drove Miller out state Highway 8 where he shot her once in the side of the head and left her on the side of the road. Police now had a suspect, a motive and a confession. But

Miller was still missing. Wooldridge said he was not familiar with the area and was not sure where he had left her body. For two days, authorities from Cass County, Texarkana, Ark., and several other agencies searched the area along state Highway 8 between Linden and Douglassville but found nothing. Wooldridge, wearing a disguise, even accompanied officers but said nothing looked familiar to him. Then on the morning of April 28, officers in a helicopter spotted a bright flash of red clothing among the leaves. Miller was finally found off of Farm to Market Road 96 near Queen City, Texas. Wooldridge's trial is scheduled for May and Attorney General Janet Reno has given her permission for prosecutors to seek the death penalty in the case.

June 1998, Wooldridge was sentenced to life without parole.

400 HOURS